Every Day in Every Way

A Year-Round Calendar
of Preschool Learning Challenges

Cynthia Holley and Faraday Burditt

Fearon Teacher Aids
Torrance, CA 90505

Linda Brandt

In memory of my father, who read me stories,
sang me songs, and taught me to play

Cindy Holley

To every member of my family, both young and old,
for their support, encouragement, and understanding

Faraday Burditt De la Camara

This Fearon Teacher Aids product was formerly manufactured and
distributed by American Teaching Aids, Inc., a subsidiary of Silver Burdett
Ginn, and is now manufactured and distributed by Frank Schaffer
Publications, Inc. FEARON, FEARON TEACHER AIDS and the FEARON
balloon logo are marks used under license from Simon & Schuster, Inc.

Designers: Diane Platner, Rose Sheifer

Illustrators: Marilyn Barr, Duane Bibby, Brad Dutsch

Copyright © 1989 by **FEARON TEACHER AIDS**
A Division of Frank Shaffer
23740 Hawthorne Blvd.
Torrance, CA 90505

ISBN 0-8224-2507-6
Printed in the United States of America

Contents

Contents

Acknowledgments

The ideas and activities in *Every Day in Every Way* come from more than 100 sources and over 25 combined years of teaching young children. We wish to thank the following individuals for their encouragement and suggestions:

Dr. Constance Champlin, Direction of Library and Media Services, Indianapolis, Indiana

Dr. John Champlin, Special Education Consultant, Council Bluffs, Iowa

Paloma Garrido, Bilingual Preschool Teacher Assistant, Madrid, Spain

Dorritt Hansen, Preschool Teacher, Copenhagen, Denmark

Constance Johnston, Speech and Language Clinician, Wilmington, Illinois

Sibley Labendiera, Kindergarten Teacher, Madrid, Spain

Diantha McBride, Librarian and Curriculum Coordinator, Madrid, Spain

Trudy Rutherford, Early Childhood Physical Education Specialist, Madrid, Spain

Donna Schreck, School Psychologist, Omaha, Nebraska

Rachel Siebert, Harvard University Doctoral Candidate, Boston, Massachusetts

Karen Walsh, Nutrition Consultant, Virginia Beach, Virginia

Introduction

Every day more children are attending preschool programs because more mothers are working and because more parents see preschool as an enriching experience that they want to offer their children. With this greater awareness of the benefits of early childhood education, preschool programs have gained a more important place in "academia."

Psychologists, researchers, and child development specialists continue to provide evidence of the influence of environmental factors on the development of young children. It has been reported that as much as half of an individual's intelligence is developed by the age of 4 and that the first 4 or 5 years are the most susceptible to environmental influences. Many leaders in early childhood education see the educational developments in the earliest years of life as the most important and the most in need of attention.

School administrators and early childhood educators have a greater responsibility than ever to reassess the role of early childhood education in the life of young children and the role of the preschool as the first link in a long chain of instruction. Success in a child's progress through school depends largely on the foundation laid in the early years.

Every Day in Every Way has been designed to help early childhood educators stimulate students of varying backgrounds, ages, and levels of achievement. Each weekly unit is built around a theme and presents daily activities to introduce or to reinforce at least ten developmental skills that lay a foundation for future academics. These skills, appropriate for introduction in classrooms of 3- to 5-year-old children, were carefully selected

after an exhaustive review of developmental skill lists and cognitively oriented curriculums as well as years of experience with young children.

Because young children have a natural curiosity and an eagerness to explore, the skills are introduced not through drill but through fun, exciting activities. These activities were field-tested at The American School of Madrid, Spain, with 3- to 5-year-old children of diverse backgrounds, nationalities, and abilities. Although the topics and materials are most relevant for children in standard preschool, day care, and kindergarten classrooms in the United States, they are also appropriate for bilingual classrooms and for those with children from other cultures. With adjustments for developmental ages, many of the activities can also be used in preschool handicapped and primary special education classrooms.

The tasks presented in this curriculum have been designed to challenge all but to bring anxiety to none. Because each class has special interests and because each child has unique needs, *Every Day in Every Way* is intended to be used with flexibility. We hope that the ideas and materials presented in this *Year-Round Calendar* will be enjoyable as well as meaningful for young children—and that they will be practical as well as informational for early childhood professionals.

How to Use This Book

With well over 1,000 ideas for teaching 135 skills in language arts, mathematics, science, social studies, music, physical education, and art, both experienced and novice teachers will find a wealth of information in *Every Day in Every Way* to guide them throughout the year. In a convenient week-at-a-glance format, the *Year-Round Calendar* provides a thematic curriculum—the "what" for teaching young children. The "why" and the "how" are found in the companion volume, *Resources for Every Day in Every Way.*

This teacher's handbook not only contains the words to the songs, rhymes, and fingerplays as well as the recipes and the patterns and worksheets recommended in the *Year-Round Calendar*, but it also spells out how to set up a preschool program that is geared to the developmental needs and abilities of young children.

In the *Year-Round Calendar* you'll find an instructional program for each school day. Each weekly unit is presented in a calendar format for easy reference, describing daily activities that introduce or reinforce at least ten targeted skills (all the skills are shown in the Index of Skills, pp. 121–125). At the top of each calendar page, you'll find the theme of the week and the skills highlighted in the week's unit. Each day's lesson plan is based on a regular daily schedule (see page 8) and includes the following categories:

- **Thinking and Talking.** Tasks for language and conceptual development, usually conducted in large groups.

- **Learning by Doing.** Concrete experiences such as experiments and cooking projects as well as follow-up paper-and-pencil tasks and visual-perception exercises. (Recipes and reproducible worksheets are in *Resources for Every Day in Every Way*.)

- **Crafts and Creations.** Arts, crafts, kitchen creations, and constructions. (Patterns for many of the crafts and constructions are in *Resources for Every Day in Every Way*.)

- **Songs and Games.** Popular songs, nursery rhymes, fingerplays, and games as well as physical explorations, exercises, and activities to develop rhythm, coordination, and balance. (Words to songs, rhymes, and fingerplays are in *Resources for Every Day in Every Way*.)

- **Recommended Resources.** Books, audiovisual materials, field trips, and community visitors to reinforce weekly themes and skills. For each week, a minimum of seven storybooks (usually traditional favorites that are readily available), two filmstrips, and two selections from record albums are suggested, and occasionally a video is noted. (At the end of this book are lists of suppliers of the materials recommended.)

Each of the 135-plus skills is highlighted in at least three weekly themes, and most are presented four or five times throughout the year. In addition to the 10 to 14 skills focused on each week, other skills are informally reinforced as well. For example, weather concepts are dealt with daily, but in certain weeks the teacher zeroes in on the skill "Identify seasonal changes."

The skills are developmentally appropriate for introduction in classrooms of 3- to 5-year-old children, although not each child will necessarily master every skill. For example, a 5-year-old will most likely balance longer on one foot "like a flamingo" than a 3-year-old, but the activity can be successfully introduced at this stage of development. An attempt has been made to present age-appropriate skills through activities that allow children of varying abilities to experience success.

The skills may be taught in sequence as presented in the *Year-Round Calendar*, or they may be taught according to the curriculum you have developed for your classroom. For example, if the local police department sends Officer Friendly to your classroom in September, refer to the Index of Skills at the back of this book. Under the heading "Social Studies," you will find the skills "Name jobs and workers in the community," "Give reasons why people work," and "Comprehend and follow basic safety rules." Note the weeks that these skills are highlighted in the *Year-Round Calendar*, and refer to them for specific activities.

The *Year-Round Calendar* is flexible. You can interchange the materials and activities to meet the needs and interest of your class. You can review skills in subsequent weeks and add others to the week's program. The skills are keyed to traditional subject areas in order to relate them to the skills taught in primary schools. (At the end of this book, you will find an index of the skills keyed to the weeks when they are presented.) You can repeat favorite songs, fingerplays, and games. You can add newly published books and filmstrips. You can select as many resources as your budget will allow. The resources recommended here have all been previewed and field-tested. They were selected on the basis of academic appropriateness, quality, efficient use of materials, and most important, an A-OK rating by young children.

The activities in the *Year-Round Calendar* can be adapted to the special interests of the each classroom. For example, a class in Miami may put less emphasis on units with snow themes and extend units with sand and water activities. A classroom with Chinese students may supplement the *Year-Round Calendar* by adding a week on Chinese New Year.

The activities suggested in this curriculum should also be adapted to the developmental level of each child. Because each classroom contains children at varying stages of development, the activities described in the *Year-Round Calendar* are designed to span ability levels and lend themselves to individualization. The educator should continually make an effort to offer activities that challenge the young child but at the same time take care to ensure that no child feels pressured to perform a task at which he or she will not succeed.

The following approaches are helpful in individualizing activities:

1. *Assist the child with the task.* The teacher could, for example, hold and turn the paper as the child cuts. The more mature child may walk the balance beam alone, but the teacher may wish to hold the hand of a less mature student.

2. *Adapt the activity.* The child could be asked to write the first letter of his or her name rather than the entire name. More mature children could be asked to name colors while less mature children could be asked to find and match circles of the same color. Younger children may learn the names of five farm animals while older children may learn the names of twelve farm animals.

3. *Substitute another activity.* If a child does not want to cut out items for the calendar, he or she could be asked to remove pictures from the old calendar on the bulletin board. While a group of mature children may show interest in learning to play T-ball, another group of children may prefer simply to throw and catch a big ball.

The key is to respect the individual capabilities and interests of each child. There are 3-year-olds who are quite interested in learning to write their names, and 5-year-olds who do not demonstrate maturity for paper-and-pencil tasks. Children should never be denied the opportunity to experience success when interested in and capable of achieving skills above standard age expectations. Equally important, young children must never feel pressure to attempt a task for which they are not capable of experiencing a degree of success.

Emphasis should be on the process, not the product. The underlying goal of the early childhood program is to provide the young child with opportunities to succeed in all areas of development. The skills and activities in *Every Day in Every Way* are designed to promote a sense of accomplishment in young children in an enjoyable manner.

The Daily Schedule

Suggested below are schedules for half-day, full-day, and extended-day programs that incorporate the five areas of activity described in the *Year-Round Calendar.*

The key to a successful schedule is a balance of activities throughout the school day. Young children need to offset active with quiet time, group with individual time, and indoor with outdoor time. The early childhood program should also provide time for open, child-directed activities in addition to the structured, teacher-directed activities. Although the *Year-Round Calendar* presents many suggestions to stimulate the young child, it is important to schedule periods each day for child-directed activities. For example, children may be directed to make animals from clay during "farm week" as a "Learning by Doing" activity, but they should also have ample opportunities to explore freely with clay and other art materials during center time.

Routines and structured times are important because preschoolers like to anticipate and repeat events. Knowing that recess generally follows rest time, for example, helps young children feel secure in their environment. The transition between periods should be smooth, and often a clue, such as flicking the lights, helps to signal the next activity.

Although a basic schedule (such as the ones suggested below) is important, timetables that are too rigid can intimidate and frustrate preschoolers. Use the schedule as a rule of thumb, but let it be flexible to allow for student interest and for special events.

Sample Schedule

Half-Day Program

9:00 Arrival, Fine-Motor Activities

9:15 Learning Centers

9:30 Opening Circle Time, Planning, Thinking and Talking

10:00 Music and Movement

10:20 Snack

10:40 Learning by Doing

11:00 Recess

11:20 Storytime

11:30 Crafts and Creations

11:50 Closing Circle Time, Rhymes, Fingerplays, and Dramatizations

12:00 Dismissal

(Cleanup following each activity as needed)

Full-Day Program

9:00 Arrival, Fine-Motor Activities

9:30 Opening Circle Time, Planning, Thinking and Talking

10:00 Snack

10:20 Learning Centers

11:00 Storytime

11:10 Learning by Doing

11:30 Recess

12:00 Lunch and Rest

1:30 Music and Movement

2:00 Crafts and Creations

2:30 Recess

3:00 Closing Circle, Rhymes, Fingerplays, and Dramatizations

3:30 Dismissal

(Cleanup following each activity as needed)

Extended-Day Program

7:30 Staggered Arrival, Outdoor Play, or Indoor Unstructured Play

8:30 Fine-Motor Activities

9:00 Opening Circle Time, Planning, Thinking and Talking

10:00 Snack and Cleanup

10:20 Learning Centers

11:00 Learning by Doing

11:20 Recess

12:00 Wash Hands, Lunch, and Rest

2:00 Storytime

2:20 Music and Movement

2:45 Crafts and Creations

3:15 Afternoon Snack

3:30 Recess

4:30 Closing Circle, Rhymes, Fingerplays, and Dramatizations

5:00 Learning Centers and Educational Television (Extended day programs often offer a short period when the children watch *Sesame Street* or another educational TV program appropriate for preschoolers.)

Staggered Dismissal

(Cleanup following each activity as needed)

The Day's Events

Arrival: The staff greets children as they enter the classroom and exchanges written or verbal communication with the parents, as necessary. Children are encouraged to hang up jackets and put lunch boxes and such in proper place.

Fine-Motor Activities: The children work independently or in small groups at work-tables stocked with such materials as puzzles, pegboards, stacking blocks, plastic snap-together toys, and clay.

Learning Centers: The children move from center to center, interacting freely with the various environments. Focuses for learning areas can include dramatic play, construction, manipulative play, language, art, and investigation. The teacher frequently changes the materials and environments and carefully monitors the children's interactions in the centers.

Recess: Weather permitting, the children go outdoors to socialize and to swing, slide, climb, and play with equipment such as balls, buckets, shovels, and hula hoops.

Storytime: The teacher reads to the children from books or tells stories with flannelboards, dramatizations, or picture books. As often as possible, the children participate in and discuss the story of the day.

Crafts and Creations: While they are developing creativity and fine-motor coordination, the children make creations to take home.

Rest Time: In a full-day program, many children will nap. Those who do not, still need a quiet time. The teacher gives them a quiet toy and plays soft music or story records in the background.

Songs and Games: The children develop large and small muscles as well as coordination, balance, and rhythm by singing, playing instruments, following exercises, and participating in movement games.

Snack and Lunch: The teacher uses these opportunities to develop language and social development by stressing good nutrition, vocabulary development, and self-care skills.

Thinking and Talking: The teacher introduces vocabulary, shares language experiences, and involves children in activities that encourage them to reason and to solve problems through making generalizations, seeing relationships, and forming conclusions. These activities can be presented through the weekly themes in the *Year-Round Calendar*.

Learning by Doing: The children participate in concrete experiences, often in small groups, such as manipulating math objects, cooking, and conducting science experiments. Many children are ready for paper-and-pencil work. (Appropriate worksheets are found in *Resources for Every Day in Every Way*.)

Cleanup: The children assist in picking up toys, wiping tables, organizing materials, and maintaining order in the classroom in general—thus developing cooperation and a sense of pride in their classroom.

Circle Time: The children gather in a circle, usually sitting on the floor, at the beginning and end of each school day. They may share news, tell stories, sing an opening and closing song that is repeated every day, enjoy rhymes, fingerplays, and dramatizations, and do calendar and weather activities. At this time children share in the planning of each day's program. During the closing circle, the day can be evaluated and the teacher can distribute reminders and communications.

Year-Round Calendar

Key to Activities and Resources

When a symbol is boxed, the recipe, song, rhyme, or worksheet can be found in the companion volume, *Resources for Every Day in Every Way.*

 = Recipes

 = Worksheets and Patterns

 = Fingerplays

 = Rhymes and Poems

 = Songs

 = Movement and Rhythm

 = Games

 = Dramatizations

 = Books

 = Records and Tape Cassettes

 = Filmstrips

 = Community Resources

 = Video Cassettes

The preacademic skills for each weekly unit are listed in the following order, with the following abbreviations, under the heading "Skills to Introduce."

- *Science (S)*
- *Social Studies (SS)*
- *Language Arts (LA)*
- *Mathematics (M)*
- *Music (Mu)*
- *Art (A)*
- *Physical Education (PE)*

SEPTEMBER: WEEK 1
Off to School

WELCOME TO MRS. BROWN'S CLASS

	Thinking and Talking	Learning by Doing	Crafts and Creations	Songs and Games	Recommended Resources
MONDAY	During circle time, one child puts on policeman's hat and goes around circle asking children, "What is your name?" Each child responds with first and last name.	Take children on walk around classroom. Explain different centers. Ask children to name materials found in each center. Review names of objects with pictures.	Demonstrate easel painting. Children take turns at easel, while the rest paint with watercolors at tables. 	How do children move in school? They sit in a circle, rest on mats, and run on the playground. What else do we do on the playground? Have children practice sitting in circle, with legs crossed. Practice other movements as well. ♪ "Good Morning to You"	*I Like School,* by Michael Mantean Visit with the crossing guard or the bus driver. Have the school nurse visit the classroom. *Will I Have a Friend?* by Miriam Cohen
TUESDAY	Why do we have rules? Go over daily schedule with pictures and chart. Introduce school rules for indoors and out. Include important items such as washing hands before eating.	Play memory game with small classroom objects. Present 6 to 8 objects. Children cover eyes, while you remove one object. Children try to guess which object is missing. 	Children make collages from last year's paper scraps, a sheet of paper, and paste. Encourage use of small amounts of paste. 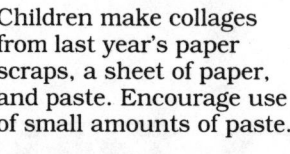	♪ "Mary Had a Little Lamb" Tell the children to pretend they are lambs. They line up behind one another and follow "Mary" to the playground.	*Shawn Goes to School,* by Petronella Breinburg "The Joy of Being You," *Kindle I,* Scholastic 

WEDNESDAY

Present 2 puppets who ask each other's name and age. Puppet then asks each child his or her name and age. Puppet can also ask for the teacher's name.

Have children arrange a group of common classroom objects from large to small. Tell the children where to put them away: "Johnny, put the ball in the basket behind the piano. Sue, put the doll in the doll bed."

 Mix a batch of *Fingerpaint Pudding.* Give each child a small cup. Have them paint a "pudding picture." Then they can lick their fingers and eat the rest with a spoon.

 "To School"

 "Follow the Leader." Have children practice climbing the stairs, walking in the halls, walking onto the playground, and so on, with one child leading the others.

 "Goodday Everybody" and "I'm Going to School Today," Ella Jenkins, *And One and Two*

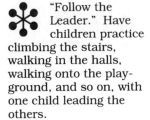 *First Things*, by George Adam

School Bus, by Donald Crews

THURSDAY

Ask children how they came to school (bus, car, foot). What did they see on their way to school?

 Give children cut-out circles for wheels to paste on outline of bus *("The Schoolbus").* They can color the bus. (Mature children can cut out their own wheels.)

Children drip several spoonfuls of various colors of tempera paint on a piece of construction paper. Fold paper in half and press on it. Open to see a colorful abstract design.

 "Two Little Hands Go Clap, Clap, Clap"

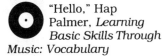 "The Bus Song"

"What Is Your Name?" Hap Palmer, *Learning Basic Skills Through Music, Vol. I*

"Hello," Hap Palmer, *Learning Basic Skills Through Music: Vocabulary*

Everybody Has a Name, by Richard Browner

FRIDAY

Take children on tour of school grounds. Introduce them to important personnel, including librarian, office secretaries, janitors, and nurse.

Take photographs of school activities. Have children arrange them in sequence. Which activity do we do first, second, next?

 How many objects can the children make with *playdough?* Help beginners learn to form balls, snakes, and other simple shapes. Make different sizes of balls and place in a row from smallest to largest.

 "My Hands"

Review playground safety rules. Discuss emergency procedures. Demonstrate and practice proper use of swings, slides, and other equipment.

 "My Name"

Billy's Treasure, by Dorothea J. Snow

 "Schoolbus Safety," *Safety Adventures of the Lollipop Dragon,* SVE

The Children's Manners Book, by Alida Allison

SEPTEMBER: WEEK 2
Me, Myself, and I

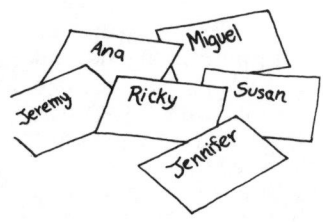

SKILLS TO INTRODUCE

- Name and describe uses of body parts (S)
- Care for personal needs (SS)
- State age and nationality (LA)
- Say first and last name (LA)
- State gender (LA)
- Recognize objects as same or different (LA)
- Manipulate laces, buttons, snaps, and zippers (LA)
- Count by rote (M)
- Compare size, weight, and volume of objects (M)
- Manipulate hands correctly for fingerplays (Mu)
- Draw and color with various mediums (A)
- Use various mediums to print (A)
- Roll body in a coordinated way (PE)

	Thinking and Talking	Learning by Doing	Crafts and Creations	Songs and Games	Recommended Resources
MONDAY	Ask children to look at one another and tell you what is the same about all of them. Point out that, despite similarities, everyone is special. Now have students look for things that are special about each of them, such as hair, eye color, nose shape, family, address, and name. Together, count eyes, noses, feet, toes, and so on.	Send home a letter asking parents' reason for giving child his or her particular name. Discuss with children how each name is special. 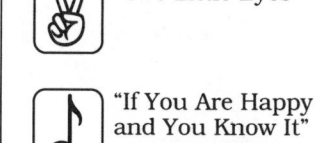	Children ink fingers with a stamp pad, and make fingerprints on paper. They can turn them into crazy critters with felt pens by drawing eyes, whiskers, legs. Examine how each child's fingerprint is special.	 "Two Little Eyes" "If You Are Happy and You Know It" 	 *I Can All by Myself* books, by Shigeo Watanabe "Hello World," *Tempo for Tots* "Walk Around the Chair" and "One and Two," Ella Jenkins, *And One and Two*
TUESDAY	Discuss different skills and abilities. Make a chart of caring for personal needs: • I can go to the bathroom alone • I can put on my shoes • I can brush my teeth • I can put on my jacket • I can open my lunchbox • I can open my thermos Count how many children can accomplish each task, and record.	Cook! Children can pretend to do lots of things, but they really can cook. Choose an individual-portion recipe, so children can produce their own culinary creations from start to finish.  Idea: *Cereal Balls*	Take an instant photo of each child. Children glue photo onto a paper square and color decorative design around border. Discuss uniqueness of faces: eye color, hair color, nose, and mouth.	"Jack and Jill" Find a grassy hill and have children take turns rolling like a log down the hill. 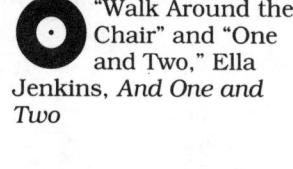	*The Little Engine That Could*, by Watty Piper "Circle Your Way" and "Birds in a Circle," Hap Palmer, *Easy Does It* "What Do I Look Like?" *Myself and Me*, Encyclopedia Britannica

WEDNESDAY

Talk about all the things we do with our bodies: walk, eat, wave, smell, throw, kick, run, hug, and so on. What body parts do we use for each activity?

Bring in various scales and balances. Weigh items. Children guess which items will weigh more. Measure and weigh the children. Graph from smallest to tallest and from lightest to heaviest. Send home each child's height and weight for parents.

Children draw faces on paper cups and staple tongue depressor inside to make puppet. They take turns asking and answering questions such as, Are you a boy? Are you a girl? Where are you from? Are you an American? Do you live in Chicago? How old are you?

 "Listening Time"

 "Drop the Hanky." Children sit in a circle. One child is "it" and walks around the circle. "It" drops the hanky behind a child, who must chase "it" around the circle and back to the hanky.

 The Story of Ferdinand, by Munro Leaf

 Dreams, by Jack Ezra Keats

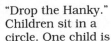 "Do You Believe in Wishes?" *Kindle I*, Scholastic

THURSDAY

Discuss likes and dislikes for kinds of food, activities, toys, places.

Children practice dressing and undressing skills with clothes in housekeeping center. They practice lifting shirt over head, buttoning buttons, zipping zippers, and so on. They dress and undress dolls.

Children make an "All About Me" book by cutting pictures from magazines and pasting them on pages with the following headings:
• Foods I Like
• People I Like
• Toys I Play With
• Things I Hate
Have each child draw a self-portrait on the cover. (Save to compare with July, Week 3, self-portrait.)

 "Wiggle"

 Line up chairs "like a train." Direct children to crawl over them and under them, to walk around them, and to sit on them.

 Pig, Pig Grows Up, by David McPhail

 "Turn Around" and "Touch," Hap Palmer, *Getting to Know Myself*

 Happy Birthday to Me, by Anne and Harlow Rockwell

FRIDAY

Bring in a small suitcase filled with favorite things from home to share with class, such as a postcard of a trip, a china animal, a sweater. Children then take turns taking suitcase home and bringing their favorite objects to share.

Have a special place on bulletin board that is decorated by a different child each week. Child can bring in photos or postcards from home or display own artwork done at home or in class.

Outline body of each child on two layers of large paper. Help children cut out and then color in facial features and clothes. Stuff with newspaper and staple. Sit "students" on chairs for parents' night.

 "Let Everyone Clap Hands with Me"

 Children do simple somersaults on rug or mat.

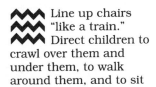

 Just Like Everyone Else, by Karla Kuskin

 Have a photographer take pictures of children. Make a video of class for parents' night.

"This Old Man," *Disney's Children's Favorites, Vol. 1*

SEPTEMBER: WEEK 3
From Head to Toe

SKILLS TO INTRODUCE

- Name and describe uses of body parts (S)
- Identify body parts (LA)
- Recall details from a story (LA)
- Identify object necessary to complete unfinished picture (LA)
- Demonstrate understanding of spatial relationships (M)
- Imitate and create rhythmic movements (Mu)
- Manipulate hands correctly for fingerplays (Mu)
- Model clay into desired shapes (A)
- Use various mediums to print (A)
- Demonstrate directional orientation (PE)
- Demonstrate dynamic and static balance (PE)

	Thinking and Talking	Learning by Doing	Crafts and Creations	Songs and Games	Recommended Resources
MONDAY	Explain that our bodies have many parts and that all bodies are different. Point to body parts on a doll, a mannequin, and self. Children imitate touching body parts. They touch body parts of doll, partner, or self, as you direct.	Children assemble puzzles of people. These can be commercial or you can make them by gluing magazine pictures onto cardboard and cutting them into pieces. Children can cut photos of themselves into 4 or 5 pieces and assemble.	On large sheet of paper, such as butcher paper, make a mural of hand- and footprints of the class. Have children dip their hands and feet in tempera paint and press on paper. Be sure to have rags and tubs or soapy water available for cleanup. 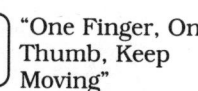	"Where Is Thumbkin?" "One Finger, One Thumb, Keep Moving"	*Gingerbread Boy* and *Little Red Riding Hood*, DLM Developmental Storybooks "Flick a Fly," Hap Palmer, *Walter the Waltzing Worm*
TUESDAY	Discuss uses of body parts. Explain that we use our body to do many things. Demonstrate an action, and have the children copy it and name the body part used: kicking, eating, waving, walking, bending, yawning, stretching, whistling, kissing, blinking, smelling.	Give each child a sheet of paper with a mirror frame drawn on it. Each child draws a picture of his or her face in "My Mirror."	Children roll, pound, squeeze, and form *playdough* into people. Faces can be drawn with sticks or dull pencils, forming features in the dough.	"Let Your Hands Go Clap" "Move Like a Fox." The fox (teacher) demonstrates a movement, and the gingerbread people (children) imitate various movements and body positions.	*A Monster Is Coming!* by Florence and Roxanne Heide *Bodies*, by Barbara Brenner "In, Out, Roundabout," *Beginning Concepts, Unit 2*, Scholastic

WEDNESDAY

Read *The Gingerbread Boy* and ask children to recall details with questions such as these: Who baked cookies? What animal was at the river? What were the gingerbread boy's eyes made of?

 Give children a worksheet that has a picture of a person who is missing various body parts (*"What's Missing?"*). The children identify and draw in the missing body parts.

 Children make handprints by pressing hand into a soft ball of *clay*, letting it dry, and painting it for a gift for the family.

 "Head, Shoulders, Knees, and Toes"

 "The Gingerbread Boy." One child is the gingerbread boy, and the others imitate the people and animals the gingerbread boy meets, while the teacher rereads the story.

Visit with an athlete. Watch a mime.

 Face Talk, Hand Talk, Body Talk, by Sue Castle

 "All Kinds of Feelings," *Kindle I,* Scholastic

THURSDAY

Show flannelboard characters for *The Gingerbread Boy.* Point to body parts on the people, the fox, and the gingerbread boy. Ask children to name the body parts and to count body parts on self and on doll or mannequin: 2 eyes, 1 nose, 10 fingernails, 10 toenails, 2 ears, 1 head.

Give children baby dolls to bathe. Have them name body parts and match clothing to appropriate body parts: socks for feet, pants for legs, hat for head, and so on.

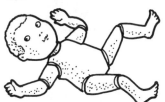

Children draw a face on a paper plate and then glue on yarn pieces for the hair.

 "Eye Winker"

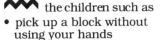 "Silly Simon Says." Give directions to the children such as
- pick up a block without using your hands
- walk without moving your knees
- talk without opening your mouth
- crawl without using your hands

 I'm Glad to Be Me, by P. K. Hallinan

 Look at Me, by Sandy Grant

 "Ears, Nose, Fingers, Toes," *Beginning Concepts, Unit 2,* Scholastic

FRIDAY

Give a circle to each child. Have children follow directions, such as "Put the circle under your foot," "Put the circle between your knees," "Put the circle under your chin," "Stand under the circle," and "Put the circle behind your back."

Show pictures of people while covering a body part with a small piece of paper. Have children identify which part is hidden behind the paper.

 Children make gingerbread people, forming a body from cookie dough (*Miss Cindy's Favorite Gingerbread People*). They can decorate with raisins. Have them name the body parts on their gingerbread people as they eat them.

 Play a record with various types of music, such as *Movin',* by Hap Palmer. Give directions to move to various rhythms such as
- stand on one foot
- walk with your hands in the air
- slowly walk backwards

 "Clapping, Clapping, Softly Clapping"

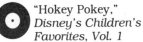 "Sam, the Tickle Man," Rosenshontz, *Tickles You!*

My Hands Can, by Jean Holzenthaler

"Hokey Pokey," *Disney's Children's Favorites, Vol. 1*

SEPTEMBER WEEK 4
Look and Listen

SKILLS TO INTRODUCE

- Name and describe uses of body parts (S)
- Name and explain use of senses (S)
- Recognize absurdities in statements (LA)
- Recognize objects as same or different (LA)
- Discriminate and identify common sounds (LA)
- Count by rote (M)
- Count up to 10 objects (M)
- Demonstrate understanding of concepts: near and far, loud and soft, and so on. (Mu)
- Paste paper and other material to make collages (A)
- Demonstrate ability in ball-handling skills (PE)
- Use playground equipment appropriately (PE)

	Thinking and Talking	Learning by Doing	Crafts and Creations	Songs and Games	Recommended Resources
MONDAY	Discuss uses of eyes and ears. How do blind and deaf people compensate? Show children a book in Braille. Have them take turns being blindfolded with a "buddy" helping them walk around the room.	Give children 3 empty baby food jars and 3 types of dried beans. Children sort "same" beans into each jar. Have the children count the beans in each of their jars. Shake jar. Do they sound the same?	Children work together to make one big collage of things we can hear. Provide magazine pictures for children to cut out and paste. 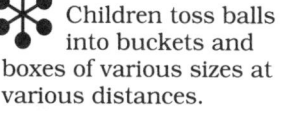	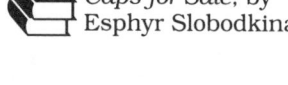 "Bow-wow Says the Dog" 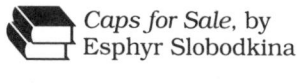 "Balls in Buckets." Children toss balls into buckets and boxes of various sizes at various distances.	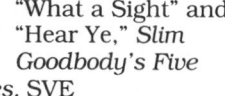 *Caps for Sale*, by Esphyr Slobodkina 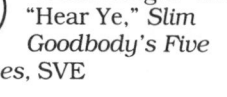 "What a Sight" and "Hear Ye," *Slim Goodbody's Five Senses*, SVE  *Goodnight Owl*, by Pat Hutchins
TUESDAY	Take children on a "looking" walk and have them take turns describing all that they see. Direct them to look for specific colors and shapes and patterns. 	Give children an assortment of finger foods on a tray, such as raisins, chips, apple slices, carrot sticks, olives, bread sticks, popcorn, cereal, grapes, and corn. Have them sort foods by color, sound, shape, size, texture. 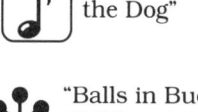 Have them use these foods to decorate a pear half and make a *Fingerfood Friend*. Eat for a snack.	Children sprinkle different colors of crayon shavings on a piece of paper and then cover with wax paper. Teacher irons with warm iron for colorful pictures.	 "Open Them, Shut Them" 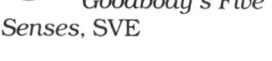 "Aiken Drum"	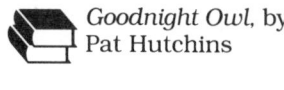 *Catching: A Book for Blind and Sighted Children*, by Virginia Allen Jensen 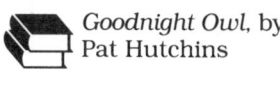 *Familiar Sounds* (tape), Developmental Learning Materials 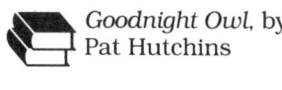 "Click," *People Who Work, Unit 2*, Scholastic

WEDNESDAY

Discuss soft sounds and loud sounds. Children take turns imitating their favorite sounds (drums, dog barking, laughing, and so on.)

Use a cardboard theater with a door, or tilt a table on its side. Put a group of objects (keys, ball, horn, etc.) "backstage." One child sits behind stage and makes a noise with each object. The other children must guess what it is.

Children make pipe cleaner spectacles.

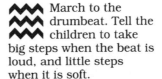

 "I Have Ten Little Fingers"

 March to the drumbeat. Tell the children to take big steps when the beat is loud, and little steps when it is soft.

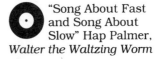 *Country Noisy Book* and *Indoor Noisy Book,* by Margaret Wise Brown

"Song About Fast and Song About Slow" Hap Palmer, *Walter the Waltzing Worm*

"Twinkle, Twinkle," *Disney's Children's Favorites, Vol. 1*

THURSDAY

Play a tape of common household, outdoor, and animal sounds and ask children to identify the sounds. Ask children absurd questions, such as, Could that be an elephant? (for a vacuum-cleaner sound).

One child leaves the room. Another hides someplace in the room with small bell. First child comes back in and tries to locate hidden child by listening for bell.

Children finger-paint, using 2 colors of *finger-paint*. They can mix with fingers to "discover" new color.

 "Foxes in Their Den"

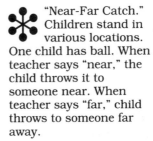 "Near-Far Catch." Children stand in various locations. One child has ball. When teacher says "near," the child throws it to someone near. When teacher says "far," child throws to someone far away.

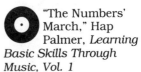 *Pigs Say Oink,* by Martha Alexander

 Listen to a musician play a guitar or other instrument.

FRIDAY

Help children count various items in classroom. Make a picture graph of the number of balls, eyes, ears, noses, or other things the children see.

Children make "viewers" by securing a piece of foil with a rubber band around end of paper towel tube. (Make sure no light enters around sides.) Poke a 1-inch circle in middle of foil. Children look through to view one object at a time.

Give children scraps of different kinds of paper: tissue paper, newspaper, construction paper. Have them listen while they crush the bits of paper before pasting them on large sheet of paper.

 "Frère Jacques" ("Are You Sleeping")

Take children to playground and discuss how eyes and ears help them stay safe. Play "Monkey See and Monkey Do," with children taking turns demonstrating the proper way to use playground equipment while classmates imitate.

 "The Numbers' March," Hap Palmer, *Learning Basic Skills Through Music, Vol. 1*

See a magician.

 1 Hunter, by Pat Hutchins

Listen to a Shape, by Marcia Brown

OCTOBER: WEEK 1
Scratch and Sniff

	Thinking and Talking	Learning by Doing	Crafts and Creations	Songs and Games	Recommended Resources
MONDAY	Discuss the senses. How are we able to smell? How are we able to feel? What part of the body do we use to taste?	Set up a smelling table. Include coffee, garlic, onion, perfume, spices, flowers, and so on.	Bring in bouquet of flowers for children to smell. Then have them paint a picture of the flowers with poster paints and cotton swabs in Impressionist style.	"Ten Little Soldiers" "Dogs and Bones." Hide "bones" made from cardboard. Children pretend they are dogs and crawl and sniff to find and collect the bones. "Senses"	*My Five Senses*, by Aliki "Lions Don't Always Roar" and "Squish and Prickles" *Experiences in Perceptual Growth*, Encyclopedia Britannica "When I Am Resting," *Tempo for Tots*
TUESDAY	Talk about things that smell good (flowers, perfume, pizza) and things that don't (skunks, diapers, rotten eggs). Children sort objects (or pictures) into two groups: good smells and bad smells.	Put objects in a surprise bag. Have children reach in and try to guess what the object is only by feeling. Have child describe object before removing it from bag.	Children make closet fresheners by sticking cloves in an orange. Hang orange on a pretty ribbon. Give each child 10 cloves, and have them count them.	"Mulberry Bush" "Hand Mimes." Children take turns going behind table turned on its side and, with only hands showing, pantomiming an emotion (happiness, sadness) or an activity (painting a picture, dancing, peeling a banana). Other children guess the mime.	*Touch Will Tell*, by Marcia Brown "Noses," Rosenshontz, *Tickles You!* "Kinds of Food," Hap Palmer, *Learning Basic Skills Through Music: Vocabulary*

WEDNESDAY	Ask children to react to different statements about senses, some true and some absurd, such as • We smell with our ears • We use our tongue to taste	Have children sort objects by texture. Count the number of soft objects, rough objects, smooth objects. Graph them pictorially. Which is the softest? smoothest? roughest? 	Children make textured domino cards to play with and take home. Have them paste material scraps on previously cut-out posterboard cards. Help children assemble finished dominoes. 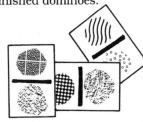	"I Touch" "I'm a Little Teapot" 	*Five Senses*, by Tasha Tudor *Where Is Everybody?* by Remy Charlip "Stone Soup," Weston Woods

THURSDAY

Name activities and have children tell you which senses we use for each one, such as painting a picture or listening to the radio.	Set up a tasting table. Blindfold children and have them guess which food they are tasting: sugar, lemon, salt, honey, and so on. 	Children model clay into favorite foods. Some may want to make a fruit or vegetable basket. Let sculptures dry, and then fire and paint with poster paints.	"Tall and Small" "The Bear Went Over the Mountain" 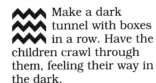 Make a dark tunnel with boxes in a row. Have the children crawl through them, feeling their way in the dark.	"Peanut Butter Sandwich," Raffi, *Singable Songs for the Very Young* *Stone Soup: An Old Tale*, by Marcia Brown

FRIDAY

Discuss what we couldn't do if one of our senses didn't function. What if we couldn't feel? What if we couldn't taste? What if we couldn't smell?	 Make *Miss Faraday's Stone Soup*. Have children feel vegetables before cutting them, and smell them before and during cooking. Have them taste vegetables before, and soup afterwards.	Make a *Glowing Garden* 	Have children climb stairs in as many ways as they can think of: hands on their head, backwards, sideways, with one leg straight, by bouncing on their bottom. "Counting Balls"	"Nothing Is Something to Do," Kindle I, Scholastic *The Little Blind Goat*, by Jan Wahl *It Looked Like Spilt Milk*, by Charles Shaw

OCTOBER: WEEK 2
Friends and Foes

SKILLS TO INTRODUCE

- Identify emotions and feelings (SS)
- Label actions (LA)
- Demonstrate understanding of abstract words (LA)
- Tell a simple story (LA)
- Demonstrate understanding of spatial relationships (M)
- Identify ordinals: first, second, third, and last (M)
- Imitate and create rhythmic movements (Mu)
- Sing class songs from memory (Mu)
- Tear and cut paper in approximate shapes and sizes. (A)
- Work with classmates on group art projects (A)
- Participate successfully in games and organized acts (PE)

	Thinking and Talking	Learning by Doing	Crafts and Creations	Songs and Games	Recommended Resources
MONDAY	Discuss friendship. How do friends help each other? Have children try to make a new friend today.	Send home letters to parents to say that children will be swapping lunches with a friend. Child asks new friend what he or she likes and then tells parents, so appropriate lunch can be made.	Each child traces his or her hand and cuts it out. All the hands are stapled together to make a "Hands That Care" necklace for a class visitor.	 Children take turns calling a friend on the telephone and inviting him or her to play. "Georgy Porgy"	 *Our Best Friends,* by Gyo Fujikawa  "Will You Be My Friend?" and "Smiles Don't Just Happen," *Kindle III,* Scholastic  *Best Friends,* by Miriam Cohen
TUESDAY	Play "Guess Who Is Missing." Line up five children. The rest of the children hide their eyes, while teacher picks one child in group of five to go out of room. The child who identifies the missing child gets to join the line!	Have children take turns being the "commander" and giving directions to other children. For example, "Go to the door!" "Stand next to the bookshelf!" "Stand on top of chair!"	Children color an entire sheet of paper with different colors and then paint over it with black paint. With 1 to 3 friends, they scratch out a picture, using a toothpick.	Children march to drumbeat and walk on tiptoe to triangle "ting." "The More We Get Together"	 *Alexander and the Terrible, Horrible, No Good, Very Bad Day,* by Judith Viorst 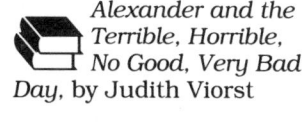 "The Sharing Song" and "The More We Get Together," Raffi, *Singable Songs for the Very Young* 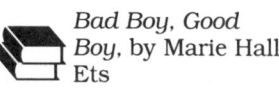 *Bad Boy, Good Boy,* by Marie Hall Ets

WEDNESDAY

Talk about good feelings and bad feelings (warm fuzzies and cold prickles). Have children give examples of actions or words that produce both types of feelings.

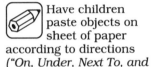 Children make *Butter.* Put a small amount of cream in a small jar. Have children take turns shaking the jar until cream forms solid butter. Spread on crackers and eat!

Children make "warm fuzzies" (cotton balls with felt eyes pasted on) and "cold prickles" (toothpicks broken and stuck in a ball of clay that hardens).

 "Question"

 Pair children and tie elastic around the wrists of partners. Play music and have children dance around the room.

 Listen to a folksinger or storyteller.

 "Feelings" and "What Do People Do," Hap Palmer, *Getting to Know Myself*

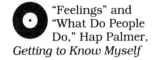 *Mine's the Best* and *It's Mine,* by Crosby Bonsall

THURSDAY

Discuss the difference between real and pretend. Give examples and have children classify by labeling as real or pretend.

 Have children paste objects on sheet of paper according to directions (*"On, Under, Next To, and In Front Of"*). Paste
- house on bottom of page
- tree beside house
- dog under tree
- car in front of house
- apples in tree

 Children make *Fingerpuppets with Feelings* showing happy, sad, angry, scared, and sleepy faces. After they color the faces and secure puppets on fingers, have them answer questions such as, Which finger has the happy face? What face does the second finger have?

 "Lavender's Blue"

 "Duck, Duck, Goose." Children sit in circle. One child walks around circle, saying "duck, duck, duck," while tapping each child's head. When tapper says "goose," the tapped child chases tapper around the circle back to home space. If tapped child catches tapper, he or she becomes new tapper.

 Take pictures or other artwork as gifts to a senior citizens' home.

 The Quarreling Book, by Charlotte Zolotow

 My Friend Is Moving, by Christine Kohler

FRIDAY

Discuss what makes people scared. Talk about scary feelings. Point out that everyone is scared of something.

Give one child the characters from a popular story such as *The Three Bears* or *The Gingerbread Boy.* Child tells story and places characters in order on flannelboard. Class reviews what happened first, second, last.

Children make monsters by tearing pieces of newspaper and pasting them on construction paper. They can add details (eyes, teeth, horns) with various pasta shapes.

 "Roses Are Red"

 "Three-legged Sack Race." Pair children. Each puts one leg into a sack with their partner. Pairs "race" to finish line. Variation: Partners lock arms back to back and try to stand up.

"Ring Around the Rosie"

 Where Is My Friend? by Betsy Maestro

Harry and the Terrible Whatzit, by Dick Gackenback

"I Don't Care Anyhow" and "Sticks and Stones," *Kindle III,* Scholastic

OCTOBER: WEEK 3
Colors of Fall

SKILLS TO INTRODUCE

- Describe weather using terms such as sunny, rainy, and cold (S)
- Identify seasonal changes (S)
- Identify basic parts of a plant (S)
- Identify and name colors (LA)
- Recognize objects as same or different (LA)
- Cut along a designated line (LA)
- Copy and create designs (LA)
- Match sets using one-to-one correspondence (M)
- Manipulate hands correctly for fingerplays (Mu)
- Create pictures, using paints (A)
- Demonstrate ability in ball-handling skills (PE)

	Thinking and Talking	Learning by Doing	Crafts and Creations	Songs and Games	Recommended Resources
MONDAY	Each day feature a color: Teacher and students dress in that color. Set up an interest center with objects of only that color. Serve a snack of that color. Color = red 	Have each child adopt a tree. Hug it; examine it; describe its parts and appearance; make bark rubbings from it with paper and crayons. Watch it change! 	Go outside and have children draw a picture of their adopted tree and color it in with soft crayons. They can cut out apple shapes and paste them on the tree.	"Apple Tree" 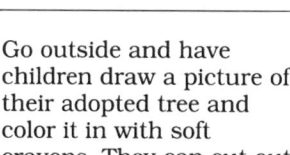 "Under the Spreading Chestnut Tree" 	📚 *The Fall of Freddie the Leaf,* by Leo Buscaglia ⊗ "Red, Blue, Yellow Too," *Beginning Concepts, Unit 1,* Scholastic
TUESDAY	Talk about changes in weather and nature that occur in the fall. Ask children why they think the leaves change color. (You'll be surprised at some of the answers.) ✏️ Make a *Weather Chart* for the week. Count the number of sunny days. Color = orange	Take a trip to a park or a neighboring woods. Give each child a paper bag to collect signs of fall in. When back at school, have them glue favorite specimens on a plastic foam tray.	Children trace around leaves. They color and then cut them out and paste on construction paper or hang from twigs to make a mobile. 	✌️ "Dancing Leaves" 〰️ Provide a variety of balls, such as: tennis, golf, football, soccer, whiffle, Ping-Pong, beach, and bowling balls. Children can see which ones bounce and which ones can roll.	📚 *Pig's Orange House,* by Ethel and Leonard Kessler 📚 *Brown Bear, Brown Bear,* by Bill Martin, Jr. 🔘 "Move Around the Color," Hap Palmer, *Easy Does It*

WEDNESDAY	Talk about wildlife activities in the fall. If possible, go outside and observe animals getting ready for winter. Color = green 	Children cover pine cones with peanut butter and sprinkle with birdseed. Hang this bird feeder with string from a tree. 	To make seed pictures, children make a design on paper with a pencil. They cover design lines with glue and stick on a selection of different seeds.	"Leaves" Play soft music and have children pretend they are leaves blown by the wind, falling softly, twirling round, gently to the ground.	Have an artist paint a picture for the children, or visit an art gallery.  "Colors," Hap Palmer, *Learning Basic Skills Through Music, Vol. 1* *The House of Four Seasons*, by Roger Duvoisin
THURSDAY	Name an object and have children state its color; for example, a banana, a ghost, grass. Bring several objects for children to sort by color into boxes or baskets. Color = yellow 	Give students a worksheet with rows of fall items (trees, leaves, pumpkins; *"Fall Favorites"*) and have them mark the different item in each row.	To make a big fall mural, draw an outline of a tree with branches. Have children paint leaves of different colors, using small pieces of sponge and poster paints.	"Five Little Leaves" "Leaping Leaves." Put cardboard leaves on the floor. Children step and leap from leaf to leaf on teacher's command—from red to green to yellow to orange to brown, and so on. Remind them not to step on the grass!	Take the class for a walk in the park. *Little Blue and Little Yellow*, by Leo Lionni *A Tree Is Nice*, by Janice May Udry
FRIDAY	What special things do we do in the fall? Make a picture chart or show pictures of fall activities. Color = blue 	Place as many apples as children in a row. Give each child a toothpick (worm) to put in an apple, to make a one-to-one correspondence. 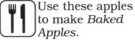 Use these apples to make *Baked Apples*.	Children collect leaves, tiny twigs, and other small nature items. Put between wax paper and iron. 	"I'm Glad" "Mary Mack"	"Blue Bird, Blue Bird, Fly Through My Window," Nancy Raven, *Hop, Skip and Sing* *Rain Makes Applesauce*, by Julian Scheer "Autumn in My Neighborhood," *The Changing Seasons*, SVE

OCTOBER: WEEK 4
Boo!

SKILLS TO INTRODUCE

- Name and explain use of senses (S)
- Identify emotions and feelings (SS)
- Name common holidays and associated traditions (SS)
- Locate hidden pictures (LA)
- Identify and name colors (LA)
- Recite simple poems and rhymes (LA)
- Count by rote (M)

- Identify basic shapes (M)
- Reproduce demonstrated pattern (M)
- Demonstrate understanding of concepts near-far, loud-soft, and so on (Mu)
- Draw and color with various mediums (A)
- Participate successfully in games and organized acts (PE)

	Thinking and Talking	Learning by Doing	Crafts and Creations	Songs and Games	Recommended Resources
MONDAY	Ask children to tell you what they know about Halloween. How do we celebrate Halloween? What things do we associate with Halloween? For example, ghosts, pumpkins, witches, black cats, bats. Have children look at a calendar and count the number of days from October 1 to Halloween.	Give children a figure-ground worksheet with haunted house and hidden items: *("Hidden Halloween Ghosts").*	Children cut out an orange construction-paper pumpkin. With crayons they draw a face. Hang together to make a pumpkin patch on large mural or bulletin board. Children color in grass on bottom.	"One, Two, Three Little Witches" "Listen to the Ghost." Teacher (the ghost) says "ooo" in different ways, from different places. Ask, "Was it long or short? Was it loud or soft? Was it near or far?" Have children imitate "spooky" Halloween sounds.	*The Goofy Ghost,* by Sharon Peters *The Witch Who Was Afraid of Witches,* by Alice Low 
TUESDAY	Put extra costumes in dress-up corner. Children take turns putting on costumes and role playing characters for class. Have a ghost talk to a witch, and so on. Ask Halloween colors: What color is a ghost, a witch, a pumpkin, a bat?	Put felt pictures of cats, pumpkins, bats, witches on feltboard *("Halloween Patterns").* Have children count each group, sort items in color sets, and name the colors. Make a pattern on the feltboard and have children identify which object comes next: • bat, witch, bat, witch, _____ • ghost, ghost, pumpkin, ghost, ghost, _____	Children make lollipop ghosts. They put a facial tissue over a lollipop and tie at neck with string. They draw 2 dots and a smile with a black marker to make face. 	"The Ghost" "Witch, Witch, Ghost." Same as "Duck, Duck, Goose" (October, Week 2, Thurs.). Children say "boo" if they catch the ghost and put the ghost in the "brew."	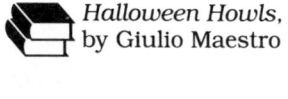 "Lollipop Dragon's First Halloween," *Holiday Adventures of the Lollipop Dragon,* SVE *Halloween Howls,* by Giulio Maestro *What's Under My Bed?* by James Stevenson

WEDNESDAY	Ask the children, What things frighten you? Are these things real or pretend? What do you want to be for Halloween? Are you really going to be that or just pretend? 	Cut out real pumpkin for a jack-o'-lantern. Have children count the seeds. Bake *Pumpkin Seeds*. Make *Witch's Brew* to drink.	With paper scraps and pieces of junk (buttons, plastic foam), children make scary masks out of large paper bags. Teacher cuts out eyeholes.	Children put on witch's hat and walk on a line with a cup of "Witch's Brew," trying not to spill it. Then they try this on a balance beam. "Ten Little Witches"	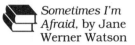 "Five Little Pumpkins," Raffi, *Singable Songs for the Very Young* *Sometimes I'm Afraid*, by Jane Werner Watson *Gus Was a Friendly Ghost*, by Jane Thayer
THURSDAY	Introduce circles and triangles and squares. Name and describe them. Have children sort and count them by attributes: • How many red shapes? • How many circles? • How many red circles? • How many red squares? • How many green circles?	 Children make witches, snowmen, vehicles, trees, caterpillars, and so on with paper shapes *("Shape-a-Picture")*. 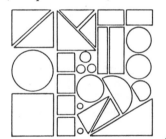	Children make patterns on cash-register tape by printing with potatoes cut into shapes and dipped in poster paints. Have them copy the teacher's patterns. 	"Jack-o'-Lantern" "The Witch's Haunted House" (to tune of "Farmer in the Dell"): • The witch takes a goon… • The goon takes a cat… • The cat takes a bat… • The bat takes a ghost… • The ghost says "Boo!"	Visit a pumpkin farm, or a store to buy a class pumpkin. *Hocus Pocus Magic Show!* by Rose Greydanus "Happy Place," Rosenshontz, *Share It!*
FRIDAY	Make a classroom haunted house. Have children make scary noises on tape. Play back and identify noises. What sense are they using? Blindfold children and let them feel cold spaghetti, peeled grapes, something sticky. Guess what it is!	Make a paper haunted house with window and doors that open. Behind each, put a Halloween character. On each window and door, put a number. Play a memory game with the children. What is behind Window #3?	Children make black construction paper bats from folded paper cut into bat wings *("Bat Pattern")*. Hang bats on rubber bands from ceiling.	"Five Little Pumpkins" Children wear costumes to school. Ask parents to bring treats. Children play "Eat the Donut" (hang it from a string) and "Bob for Apples." Have a Halloween parade!	"Winnie the Witch and the Frightened Ghost," *Fran Allison's Autumn Tales of Winnie the Witch*, SVE 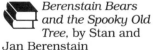 *Berenstain Bears and the Spooky Old Tree*, by Stan and Jan Berenstain

NOVEMBER: WEEK 1
All in the Family

	Thinking and Talking	Learning by Doing	Crafts and Creations	Songs and Games	Recommended Resources
MONDAY	Discuss the meaning of the word *family*. Identify different people who make up a family. Invite family members to visit the classroom and share family traditions and stories with the children. Have the visitors share a favorite song or book with the class.	Record voice of various representative family members. Play tape and have children identify each voice: a mother, a baby, a brother, and so on. 	Children draw pictures of their own families. Teacher covers pictures with clear plastic and adds construction paper frame. Children decorate the frame with a pattern of their choice. 	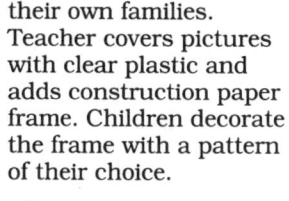 "Grandmother's Glasses" "The Three Bears." Read the story, then give children props such as construction paper bear ears, bowls for porridge, and chairs. Retell story and have children take turns acting out characters.	*The Three Bears,* DLM Developmental Storybooks "Mira, Mira, Marisol" and "Happy Birthday, Howard," *Five Children,* Scholastic *My Mom Travels a Lot,* by Caroline Bauer
TUESDAY	Children bring photos of their families and introduce each member in the photo to their classmates. Discuss the relationships of these people to the child: aunt, mother, sister, father, and so on. What do these people do in the family?	Provide clothing and props so that children can dress up like various family members. Let children role play morning routines with shaving cream, and popsicle stick "razors," hair rollers, empty makeup kits, mirrors, and so on. Direct children to move to various positions: brother stand beside grandmother, sister sit on floor behind baby brother, and so on.	Children collect leaves of various sizes: a baby leaf, a mother leaf, a father leaf, and leaves for other family members. They paste them onto construction paper, and if they wish, draw arms, legs, and faces to create a leaf family.	Have children imitate movements of family members. For example, crawl like a baby, run like a teenager, skip like a 7-year-old. "Mother, May I?" "Mother" gives commands such as "take 3 big steps," "take 2 baby steps." Children who forget to ask "Mother, may I?" must return to start.	*Let's Find Out About Families,* by Valerie Pitt *Daddy Makes the Best Spaghetti,* by Anna Grossnickle Hines  See a puppet show or show a family's "home movie."

WEDNESDAY

Discuss the roles of individual members of a family. Name ways children can help in families. Name activities that families participate in together.

 Give each child a worksheet with a maze *("Brother to Sister Maze")* and *("Sister to Brother Maze")*. Have children follow the maze without taking pencil off the road. Use a simple "maze" for the youngest children.

Make family puzzles by having each child paste a large magazine picture of a family or a family member on cardboard. Cut the cardboard into 4 to 6 pieces to make a puzzle.

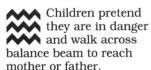

 "Fine Family"

 Children pretend they are in danger and walk across balance beam to reach mother or father.

 Are You My Mother? by Philip D. Eastman

Noisy Nora, by Rosemary Wells

 "Boogie Woogie Bear," *Preschool Fitness*

THURSDAY

Make statements about families and have students decide if they are true or false and answer yes or no accordingly; for example, "Mothers are usually 2 years old," "Baby brother drives an airplane to work," "Grandfather is a man."

 Make patterns on a flannelboard using felt family member cut-outs *("Family Members")*. Have children try to reproduce the same pattern below the teacher's: sister, mother or father, father, grandfather. Have children create their own patterns for other classmates to copy with these flannelboard cut-outs.

 Children make fingerpuppet families from *Edible Peanut Butter Playdough*. They can decorate faces with raisins and Fruit Wrinkle pieces. Eat for a snack.

 "He's Got the Whole World"

 "Family Charades" Children take turns role playing various family members. Others ask questions such as Are you a boy? Are you old? and try to guess the family member.

We're Good Friends, My Brother and I, by P. K. Hallinan

A Baby Sister for Frances, by Russell Hoban

Our New Baby, by Jane Hamilton-Merritt

FRIDAY

Ask children to locate the biggest person in their family picture. Also have them find the oldest, smallest, strongest, youngest, blondest, and so on. Have children identify which members are male and which are female.

Children make pairs of family game cards by cutting out pictures of family members from duplicate magazines and pasting them on cardboard cards. Divide children into groups and play Concentration.

Hang a big map of the U.S. or the world on the wall. Children draw a picture on a small paper flag of a relative who lives far away. Pin these flags in appropriate locations on the map.

 "Brother, Come and Dance with Me"

 "Five Little Babies"

 "Five Little Ducks"

 "It Takes Two" and "It's OK," Rosenshontz, *Tickles You!*

 *My Mother Says There Aren't Zombies, Ghosts, Vampires, Creatures, Demons, Monsters, Fiends, Goblins, and Thieves*, by Judith Viorst

 "Together," "Chinatown," and "Piñata," *Five Families*, Scholastic

NOVEMBER: WEEK 2
No Place Like Home

SKILLS TO INTRODUCE

- Match common objects found in home to appropriate location (SS)
- Identify different types of homes (SS)
- Recite address and telephone numbers (LA)
- Sequence events from a story (LA)
- Identify object necessary to complete unfinished picture (LA)
- Discriminate and identify common sounds (LA)
- Identify top, middle, and bottom of objects (M)
- Reproduce basic shapes (M)
- Demonstrate understanding of concepts: near and far, hard and soft, and fast and slow (Mu)
- Create constructions using 3-D materials (A)
- Perform climbing skills (PE)

	Thinking and Talking	Learning by Doing	Crafts and Creations	Songs and Games	Recommended Resources
MONDAY	Using large pictures, discuss function of home (shelter). What different types of homes are there? (apartments, trailers, igloos, tents, houseboats, condominiums, lighthouses, and so on)	Children put felt people in various positions around a feltboard house (*"Family Members"* and *"House Pattern"*) on top of, in middle of, below, next to, and at bottom of house.	Get several large appliance boxes and cut holes for doors and windows. Children divide into "families" (small groups) and paint their houses with tempera paint. Cut curtains from old pillowcases.	"Houses" Cut openings of different shapes in large box or board. Have children throw beanbags through the openings. Give directions such as "throw the beanbag through the top circle, through the bottom square."	*Houses* and *How We Live*, by Anita Harper "Triangle, Circle, and Square" and "One Shape, Three Shapes," Hap Palmer, *Learning Basic Skills Through Music, Vol. II* "Follow the Architect's Plan," *People Who Work, Unit 2*, Scholastic
TUESDAY	Discuss materials that homes can be made of (brick, concrete, wood, ice, animal skins, stone, metal, and so on). Why do you think these materials are chosen? (price, availability, usefulness) What materials did the three little pigs use for their houses? Which house did the big bad wolf visit first, second, last? What happened at the last house?	Children glue toothpicks onto construction paper to make a house. They may enjoy drawing household items or people in the rooms of the house. 	Draw a big outline of house for wall mural. Divide into rooms. Children cut out magazine pictures and paste in appropriate rooms.	Children make pyramids with 3 to 5 people. Children act out story of "The Three Little Pigs." 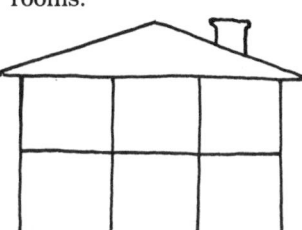"Bingo's Doghouse"	*The Three Pigs* and *Hansel and Gretel*, DLM Developmental Storybooks "Boxes, Clocks, Building Blocks," *Beginning Concepts, Unit 1*, Scholastic

WEDNESDAY

 What is an address? Why do we each have one? Encourage children to learn their address.

 Give *certificates* to children when they can say their phone number and address.

 Give children a worksheet that has houses with missing parts (*"Complete the Houses"*). Have children fill in the missing parts, reproducing shapes.

 Children make *Rainbow Toast* houses from bread that has been painted with a milk and food color solution and toasted.

 Children imitate how we go from the top to bottom of a building by climbing stairs and ladders. Pretend to be elevators: squat and slowly stretch up high, counting the floors. Return to "ground floor."

 "Old Mother Hubbard"

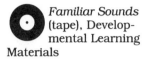 *Everybody Has a House,* by Mary McBurney Green

Familiar Sounds (tape), Developmental Learning Materials

Oh, Were They Every Happy, by Peter Spier

THURSDAY

Show pictures of different rooms in a house. Discuss what activities are carried out in each room. Talk about the need for stairs, elevators, and ladders in a house.

Play a tape of common household sounds such as a toilet flushing, a mixer, a vacuum cleaner, and a doorbell. Have children listen and identify.

Children make an "apartment building." Each child decorates a shoe box apartment. Pile them high against a wall to make a tall complex. Point out top and bottom floors.

 "Two Little Houses"

 "Go In and Out the Window"

 The Napping House, by Audrey Wood

 Visit the city to look at all the buildings in which people live.

FRIDAY

Show pictures of different rooms. Talk about objects found in each room.

Put picture labels on shoe boxes to denote different rooms of the house. Have children put pictures of objects in appropriate "room."

Children make igloos with sugar cubes and white glue.

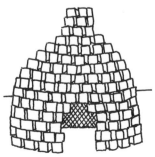

 "There Was an Old Woman"

"Big Bad Wolf Tag." Tie a bell around the "big bad wolf." Can you hear him coming? Is he near? Use a cardboard house for "base."

 Building a House, by Byron Barton

 "Who's Afraid of the Big Bad Wolf?" Rosenshontz, *Share It!*

The Cow in the Kitchen, by Evelyne Johnson

NOVEMBER: WEEK 3
Munch and Crunch

SKILLS TO INTRODUCE

- Distinguish between healthy and junk foods (S)
- Categorize common foods (S)
- Discriminate objects tactilely (S)
- Use comparative and superlative adjectives (LA)
- Associate objects by given attributes (LA)
- Recall and name objects removed from a set (LA)
- Sort and classify objects into sets (M)
- Compare size, weight, and volume of objects (M)
- Manipulate hands correctly for fingerplays (Mu)
- Model clay into desired shapes (A)
- Paste paper and other materials to make collages (A)
- Participate successfully in games and organized acts (PE)

	Thinking and Talking	**Learning by Doing**	**Crafts and Creations**	**Songs and Games**	**Recommended Resources**
MONDAY	What is food? Why do we need it? Show children different objects. Ask them if the object is food or not.	Fill a shopping bag with foods as the children watch. Then have them name what you "bought." See how many items they can recall.	Cook spaghetti, using one tablespoon oil to prevent sticking. Drain and toss in bowls with glue and various colors of food coloring. Children make spaghetti creations in styrofoam trays. Dry 2 days, remove from tray, and hang with yarn. 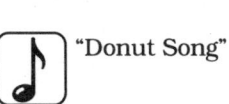	"Here Are My Lady's Knives and Forks" "Donut Song" "I Eat My Peas with Honey"	*Mr. Rabbit and the Lovely Present,* by Charlotte Zolotow Visit the school kitchen. Take a trip to a bakery or restaurant. "Bumpy-Lumpy," *Beginning Concepts, Unit 1,* Scholastic
TUESDAY	Discuss where food comes from. Where do bread, meat, vegetables, fruit, and milk come from? 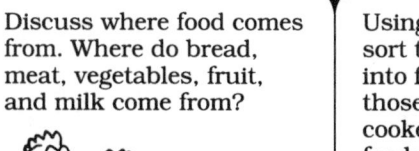	Using real food, children sort them by color, then into foods eaten raw and those that must be cooked, and finally into foods with and without seeds.	 Children model *clay* into fruit or vegetable shapes and make a clay basket. Put clay fruit into basket. Let dry. Let children paint with poster paints.	"My Father Owns the Butcher Shop" Children see how many kernels of popcorn they can drop into a milk bottle.	*Let's Eat,* by Gyo Fujikawa Have a chef visit and demonstrate a meal. "Raisins and Almonds," Ella Jenkins, *And One and Two*

W E D N E S D A Y	Discuss the different food groups (dairy, meat, grain, fruit–vegetable). Put one food for each food group out in front of children. They hide their eyes and you remove one. Which food (or food group) is missing?	Using shoe boxes labeled with one of the four food groups, children put food pictures into correct food group box. 	Children draw picture of a healthy meal (one food from each group) on a paper plate. Paste on construction-paper placemat along with napkin, plastic cup, and silverware.	 "Pat-a-Cake" "Hot Potato." Use a real baking potato. Pass the potato to music. When the music stops, the child who is holding it is "cooked."	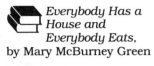 *Everybody Has a House and Everybody Eats,* by Mary McBurney Green "Ten Green Apples," Ella Jenkins, *Growing Up with Ella Jenkins*

T H U R S D A Y	What we eat can affect the way we feel. How would we feel if we just ate candy and sweets? If we ate healthy foods from the four food groups? 	Bake *Quickest Bread.* Point out which food groups are included in the recipe. 	Make a large wall mural of healthy and junk foods. Divide paper with line. Children cut out magazine pictures of foods and paste on appropriate half.	"Jelly"
				  "Pease Porridge Hot"
				  Tell story of "The Little Red Hen" as children dramatize it with props. Class chants in unison "I won't" each time the Little Red Hen asks for help.
					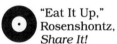 *The Vegetable Thieves,* by Inga Moore
					  "Eat It Up," Rosenshontz, *Share It!*
					 Eating Out, by Helen Oxenbury

F R I D A Y	Put a fruit or vegetable into a sock. One child reaches in, feels the food, and describes it to the others. The child who correctly names the hidden food can take the next turn.	Set up balance scale. Have children guess which fruit or vegetable is heavier, lighter, the heaviest, the lightest. Weigh to find out.	Children paste torn pieces of red tissue or construction paper inside outline of large apple on construction paper. They then glue a twig for the stem and a real leaf. 	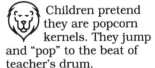 "Jack Spratt" Children pretend they are popcorn kernels. They jump and "pop" to the beat of teacher's drum. 	*The Little Red Hen,* by Paul Galdone *There Was an Old Woman,* by Steve Kellogg 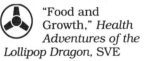 "Food and Growth," *Health Adventures of the Lollipop Dragon,* SVE

NOVEMBER: WEEK 4
Turkey Time

	Thinking and Talking	Learning by Doing	Crafts and Creations	Songs and Games	Recommended Resources
MONDAY	Tell or read the Thanksgiving story. How were things different a long time ago? How do we celebrate Thanksgiving now? 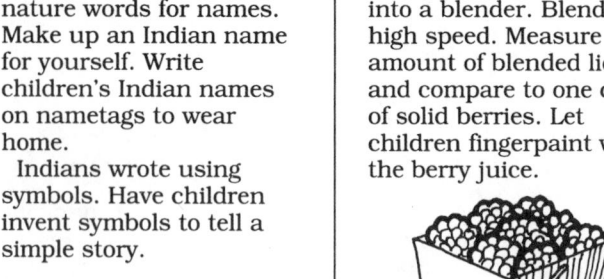	Use feltboard to have children match teepees to Indians, turkeys to Pilgrims, and so on *("Thanksgiving Patterns")* and tell you if the sets are equal or if one has more members. Count and compare.	Children cut and fringe large feathers of different colors of construction paper. Write numbers on feathers. Children paste them onto big turkey on wall mural in numerical order. "What number comes after 3? Yes, Billy, you have 4."	 "Thanksgiving Friends"  "Ten Little Indians"	 *Pilgrim Children Come to Plymouth,* by Ida Delage 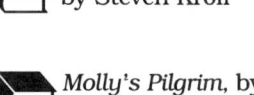 "Squanto and the First Thanksgiving," *Fall Holiday Celebrations,* SVE 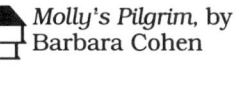 Visit a farm with turkeys.
TUESDAY	Discuss how the Indians lived. They often used nature words for names. Make up an Indian name for yourself. Write children's Indian names on nametags to wear home. Indians wrote using symbols. Have children invent symbols to tell a simple story.	Measure one cup of blueberries or raspberries into a blender. Blend on high speed. Measure amount of blended liquid and compare to one cup of solid berries. Let children fingerpaint with the berry juice. 	Children make placemats by weaving 1-inch strips of different colors of construction paper into a large sheet of construction paper that has slits 1 inch apart cut to 1 inch of top and bottom. Staple ends of strips. Use for Thanksgiving feast.	 "Ten Fat Turkeys"  Children creep and crawl on stomachs like "Indians."	 *One Tough Turkey,* by Steven Kroll 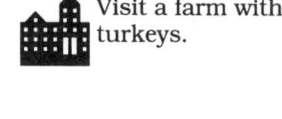 *Molly's Pilgrim,* by Barbara Cohen 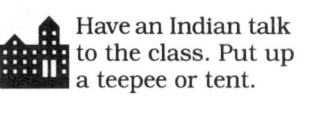 Have an Indian talk to the class. Put up a teepee or tent.

WEDNESDAY

What things are you thankful for? What does *thankful* mean? What does *happy* mean? Were the Pilgrims brave? Were the Indians kind?

 Give children worksheet with dot-to-dot picture of a teepee ("Dot-to-Dot Teepee").

Children make a Thanksgiving number book. Depending on children's ability level, you or they write a number at top of each page of stapled book. Children draw appropriate number of objects, such as 1 pumpkin pie, 2 teepees, 3 seeds, 4 pumpkins.

 "The Turkey"

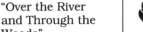 "Over the River and Through the Woods"

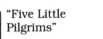 "Five Little Pilgrims"

 "It's Mine," *Kindle III*, Scholastic

 Cranberry Thanksgiving, by Wende and Harry Devlin

 Arthur's Thanksgiving, by Marc Brown

THURSDAY

Show a calendar and count the number of days from Nov. 1 to Thanksgiving. Count in "big Indian chief" voices and in "quiet Pilgrim" voices. Say the days of the week together.

Teacher cuts cross, triangle, and V shapes into potato halves. Children dip potatoes into tempera paint and, working from left to right, make Indian patterns across strips of paper. Children paste these strips onto an oatmeal carton to make a drum. They can also use one strip for a headband and add as many construction paper feathers as they wish.

Children make Pilgrim and Indian villages with teepees and cabins. For log cabins, they glue pretzels onto milk cartons. For teepees, they decorate 12-inch circles that have been slit from edge to center. Staple together and cut entrance flap.

 "Five Big Indians"

 Children make and play instruments. "Indian shakers" can be made with beans inside 2 paper plates stapled together. "Drums" can be made from oatmeal cartons.

 "Maori Indian Battle Chant," Ella Jenkins, *You'll Sing a Song*

 Little Bear's Thanksgiving, by Janice

"Yah-a-Tay," *Five Families*, Scholastic

FRIDAY

Children act out the Thanksgiving story while teacher narrates. Talk about foods. What do we eat at Thanksgiving? In what order? When do we eat pies?

Have a Thanksgiving feast. Parents contribute several items to share with the children.

 The class bakes *Pumpkin Pie*.

Children string Fruit Loops, Cheerios, or painted macaroni to make an Indian necklace.

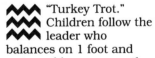 "Creeping Indians"

"Turkey Trot." Children follow the leader who balances on 1 foot and trots and hops across the room.

 "One Potato, Two Potato"

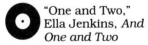 *Hard Scrabble Harvest*, by Dahlov Ipcar

 "One and Two," Ella Jenkins, *And One and Two*

"She'll Be Comin' Round the Mountain" and "Ten Indians," *Disney's Children's Favorites, Vol. 1*

DECEMBER: WEEK 1
Puff and Spot

SKILLS TO INTRODUCE

- Discriminate animal sounds (S)
- Identify and name pets and farm and zoo animals (S)
- Select and name opposites (LA)
- Label actions (LA)
- Recall details from a story (LA)
- Recognize numerals: 1, 2, 3, 4, 5, . . . (M)
- Match numeral to the number of a set (M)
- Sing class songs from memory (Mu)
- Paste paper and other materials to make collages (A)
- Creep and crawl in various ways (PE)

	Thinking and Talking	Learning by Doing	Crafts and Creations	Songs and Games	Recommended Resources
MONDAY	How is a pet different from other animals? Show pictures of different animals and ask, Could this animal be a pet? Why? Why not?	Put numerals on goldfish-shaped construction paper with paper clip. Children fish with string and magnet. What number did you catch? 	Children paste material scraps within outline of *Calico Cat*. Add buttons for eyes, yarn for mouth, toothpicks for whiskers.	"I Love Little Pussy" "Copycats." Teacher performs an action. Children name it and copy it; for example, eating soup, jumping rope, ironing.	*The Kitten's ABC*, by Clare Turbay Newberry *A Cat Can't Count*, by Blossom Budney "Put Your Hands Up in the Air," Hap Palmer, *Learning Basic Skills Through Music, Vol. I*
TUESDAY	How do we care for pets? Can they care for themselves? What foods do they eat? Where do animals live?	Label "dog dishes" wth numerals 1 to 5. Give children bone-shaped doggy biscuits. They put correct number of doggy bones in numbered dishes.	Make tissue paper fish *("Goldfish Pattern")*. Children staple halfway around 2 pieces of tissue paper and stuff with more tissue. Help them staple closed and apply glue and glitter for eyes. Hang fish from ceiling.	"Kitten Is Hiding" "Dog and Bone." One child leaves room. Another child is given "bone" to hide. First child returns and rest sing: "Doggie, doggie, where's your bone? Someone took it from your home!" Child gets 3 guesses to find out who.	*Where's Spot?* by Eric Hill "Baby Pet Animals," *Baby Animals in Rhyme and Song*, SVE Visit a pet store or bring pets to school for a day.

WEDNESDAY

Make up a story about "Bingo" where he lived, what he did, what he looked like. Ask questions and see if the children can recall the events.

Bring goldfish to school for the day.

 Give children a picture of a goldfish bowl ("Goldfish Bowl"). They color or paint the water blue and paste on goldfish crackers according to the number written at the top of page. Eat leftovers for snack!

 Give children picture of *Spot* the dog. Children paint black spots on dog with black shoe polish applicator or small round sponge dipped in tempera paint.

 "Five Kittens"

 "Bingo"

 Have You Seen My Cat? by Eric Carle

 Have a veterinarian talk to the class.

 The Rain Puddle, by Adelaide Holl

Animals in Verse, SVE

THURSDAY

Play a tape of animal sounds. Have children identify animal and tell whether it could be a pet.

Children bake *Perfect Peanut Butter Cookies* in the shape of dog bones.

Children make cardboard turtles ("Turtle Pattern"). Put string through the center and have turtle races.

"Do Your Ears Hang Low?"

 Children imitate animal movements: walk like a duck, run like a dog, swim like a fish, fly like a bird, crawl like a snake, hop like a rabbit, crawl like a turtle.

 "The Opposite" and "Sammy," Hap Palmer, *Getting to Know Myself*

 Dear Zoo, by Rod Campbell

"Animal Sounds," *Tempo for Tots*

FRIDAY

Children take turns pretending to be animals moving: crawling, running, stretching, padding, wagging, flying, scampering, hopping. Others identify the action and name the animal being imitated. Show pictures of animals moving. "What is the horse doing? The horse is galloping."

Teacher makes a statement; children make the opposite statement. For example, "The dog is in the house" and "The dog is out of the house." Teacher gives a command and children do opposite.

Draw a big pet store window. Children cut out pets from magazines and paste into the window.

 "Animal Poem"

 Children pretend they are horses and trot, gallop, and race across a field or around a track.

"The Old Gray Cat"

 Pssst Doggie! by Ezra Jack Keats

"Pet Sounds," Rosenshontz, *Share It!*

 *Tom and Tabby,* by Hans Peterson

"Pets for Sale," *People Who Work, Unit 2,* Scholastic

DECEMBER: WEEK 2
Teddy Bears, Dolls, and Robots

	Thinking and Talking	Learning by Doing	Crafts and Creations	Songs and Games	Recommended Resources
MONDAY	Children bring their favorite teddy bear, doll, or robot to class. Do they have names? Who gave toy to child? Give a ribbon to each child's toy: "The Fattest Bear," "The Shiniest Robot," "The Softest Doll."	Children sort their toys by kind, color, size (from smallest to largest). 	Children make felt puppets *("Hand Puppet Pattern")*. Have a few children at a time give a puppet show. 	"Fuzzy Wuzzy" "Teddy Bear" Children make kazoos by securing small square of cloth around end of toilet-tissue roll with a rubber band. Hum favorite tunes.	*Corduroy,* by Don Freeman "Corduroy," Kimbo "Touch" and "Shake Something," Hap Palmer, *Getting to Know Myself* *Alphabears,* by Kathleen Hague
TUESDAY	Is a toy alive? Even if it can move, is it alive? Show pictures of living and nonliving things. Have children identify which is which. 	Put out a group of 5 to 10 toys. Children cover eyes while you remove one toy. Children then say which toy is missing.	Children make puzzles by pasting a large magazine picture of a toy on cardboard and then cutting into 6 to 8 pieces. Children do each other's puzzle.	"Pop Goes the Weasel" Play "The March of the Toys" from *The Nutcracker Suite.* Have children move to the music like toys. Play a soft lullaby. Children quietly listen and rock their "babies" to sleep.	*Peabody,* by Rosemary Wells "Boogie Woogie Bear," *Preschool Fitness* *Ask Mr. Bear,* by Marjorie Flack

WEDNESDAY

What is a robot? What makes a robot move? What kind of language does a robot understand? Teacher can act out part of robot, while children give commands.

 Give children worksheet with hidden toys to trace *("Find the Toys")*.

Children make robots out of milk cartons, detergent bottles, and construction paper. Provide scraps of foil, bottle caps, wire pieces, pop-top lids, and such to decorate. (Carefully monitor children when they are handling anything that might be sharp.)

 "Five Little Bears"

 Fill glasses with different amounts of water. Have the children gently tap them and listen to the different tones. Children tiptoe to the sound.

 "Rag Doll"

 The Robot Birthday, by Eve Bunting

 Visit a toy store.

 Teddy, by Greta Janus

THURSDAY

 Make 3 rows of toys on feltboard *("Toy Patterns")*. Ask children to tell you which toy is on top of ball, which is next to doll, and so on.

 Give children a paper with an outline of a teddy bear and small squares of brown tissue paper *("Teddy Bear")*. Then paste squares to fill in bear. More advanced children can wrap paper around pencil eraser, dip into glue, and make stand-up fur, working from top to bottom. At bottom of page, write the bear's name as child dictates.

Children make jack-in-the-boxes. Put face on paper circle. Paste face on folded strips of paper. Squash down and paste inside mystery door, which is held closed with brad. Open and up he jumps.

 "Jack-in-the-Box"

 Children pretend they are jack-in-the-boxes and "pop" out of cardboard box. Children pretend they are rag dolls and lay relaxed on the floor.

 Have a costumed bear, Mickey Mouse, Big Bird, or Snoopy visit the classroom.

 "Rag Doll," Hap Palmer, *Pretend*

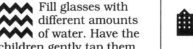 *William's Doll*, by Charlotte Zolotow

"Stitch 'n' Stuff," *People Who Work, Unit 1*, Scholastic

FRIDAY

Have each child hold a toy. Give commands such as
• put your toy beside you
• put your finger in top of toy
• put your toy under your chair

 Children make *Pooh Pancakes*. Decorate with raisins.

Give children a large sponge cut into shape of a teddy bear. Children dip into brown paint and make bears. When dry, children dribble glue for eyes, nose, mouth. Sprinkle with coffee grounds.

 "Baby's Toys"

 Children sit on floor with legs apart and roll ball to each other. Tell them to move farther and farther apart. Tell them to throw the ball up and catch it.

Winnie the Pooh, Walt Disney

Cully Cully and the Bear, by Mary Q. Steele

Push Pull, Empty Full, by Tana Hoban

DECEMBER: WEEK 3
Happy Holidays

	Thinking and Talking	Learning by Doing	Crafts and Creations	Songs and Games	Recommended Resources
MONDAY	Talk about holidays. Why are they special? What holidays can you name?	Give children outline of candy cane on red construction paper. With white shoe polish (squeeze applicator) they make white stripes. Children can cut out candy canes when dry. 	Make a wall mural with chimney and Christmas tree. Have children paint it. Staple together two paper stocking patterns *("Christmas Stocking Pattern").* Children glue cotton balls along top and write initials or name with glue and glitter. Hang stockings on chimney.	"Five Little Presents" "Rudolph, the Red-Nosed Reindeer." Children jump over a foot-high stick, leaping like reindeer.	*Bah! Humbug?* by Lorna Balian *The Night Before Christmas,* by Clement Moore "The Circle" and "The Circle Game," Hap Palmer, *Getting to Know Myself*
TUESDAY	Read or tell the story of Hanukkah. Talk about Hanukkah traditions. 	Give children a worksheet with picture of menorah *("Menorah").* Have them count the number of flames on menorah and color them with a yellow felt-tip pen.	Children make menorah by pasting bottle caps on strip of cardboard. Put small amount of playdough in each holder for candle.	"Hanukkah Candles" Teacher stands in back of room and plays instruments. Children say if loud or soft, fast or slow, high or low, long or short, same or different. Children march to music.	"Rudolph the Red-Nosed Reindeer" *Rudolph the Red-Nosed Reindeer Stories,* SVE *I Love Hanukkah,* by Marilyn Hirsh "Morris' Disappearing Bag," Weston Woods

WEDNESDAY	How do we know when holidays are? What is a date? Say days of week, months of year together. Show a calendar. Count days from Dec. 1 to Christmas. Share an advent calendar. Note important dates on the calendar by placing stickers or drawing pictures.	Bring in an assortment of ornament balls. Children sort by color and count how many are in each set. Demonstrate a pattern, and have children name which color should come next in the sequence.	Children make dreidels by cutting a circle out of construction paper and putting toothpick in the middle *("Dreidel Pattern")*. 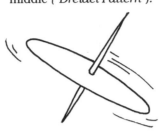	"Five Little Bells"  "My Dreydl." Children pretend they are dreidels and spin around the room.	*Chicken Soup with Rice*, by Maurice Sendak *Hanukkah Money*, by Uri Shulevitz Go to a shopping mall to see all the decorations. Buy a Christmas tree.
THURSDAY	Read or tell the story of Christmas. What traditions go with the celebration of Christmas? 	Make *Latkes*. Have children count them. 	Children cut out a large Christmas tree from green construction paper *("Christmas Tree")*. They can color ornaments or glue on Fruit Loops cereal rings to decorate. 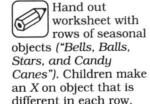	"Santa" "Up on the Housetop." Cover a chair or table with paper to look like a chimney. Children take turns jumping off the chimney.	"My Dreidel," Raffi, *Singable Songs for the Very Young* Have someone bring a menorah and discuss Hanukkah. *Laughing Latkes*, by M. B. Goffstein
FRIDAY	Ask for volunteer to retell the story of Hanukkah or Christmas with the help of teaching pictures. Have the children tell a puppet how they would like to celebrate their holiday.	Hand out worksheet with rows of seasonal objects *("Bells, Balls, Stars, and Candy Canes")*. Children make an *X* on object that is different in each row.	Give children colored paper, crayons, glitter, glue, stencils, and scissors. Let them cut out and decorate ornaments to paste on mural *("Ornament Patterns")*. They can cut long strips to make paper chains to hang across the top of mural also.	"Christmastime" "Jingle Bells" Children take turns playing the bells, passing them around circle, as they sing.	"Must Be Santa," Raffi, *Singable Songs for the Very Young* *Potato Pancakes All Around*, by Marilyn Hirsh "Hanukkah Hotcakes," SVE

DECEMBER: WEEK 4
Here Comes Santa Claus

	Thinking and Talking	Learning by Doing	Crafts and Creations	Songs and Games	Recommended Resources
MONDAY	Ask parents to visit class to share how they celebrate the holidays. Prepare questions with children beforehand: Who comes to your house? What do you eat?	Children make holiday greeting cards, using glue, glitter, markers, scissors, and construction paper as desired. Children write first name in each one. Less mature children can write their first initial. 	Make Christmas wreaths. Spray-paint different shapes of pasta green and gold. Children paste on paper plate with center cut out. Decorate with red ribbon bow.	"The Chimney" Children pretend they are resting elves and lie quietly listening as teacher plays instrumental recordings of *The Nutcracker Suite*, Handel's *Messiah*, or *Peter and the Wolf*.	*Cranberry Christmas*, by Wende and Harry Devlin *Raffi's Christmas*, Raffi *It's Really Christmas*, by Lillian Hoban
TUESDAY	Talk about giving and receiving presents. Is it fun doing both? What presents would you like to receive? Presents (including promises of "favor") can be made. 	Put out 2 groups of toys. Ask children to match or count to determine which group has more or if they are equal. Repeat with different groups of toys. Children find hidden toys in a worksheet (*"Lost Toys"*)	Help children make *clay* picture frames in oval shape. Children paint with poster paints. Paint over when dry with shellac. Put in photo taken at school of each child as present for parents. Sponge paint with holiday shapes on butcher paper for wrapping presents.	"O Christmas Tree" "Pass the Package." Children play "Hot Potato" with a package. Child with package when music stops is the "elf."	*The Christmas Doll*, by Wendy Parker "The Night Before Christmas," SVE Take children to a nursing home to sing Christmas songs and spread holiday cheer.

WEDNESDAY	Play "I Spy." Say, "I see something red." Children ask questions to find out what object is: Is it big? Is it on the Tree?	Make patterns with paper or flannel holiday shapes. Children take turns extending patterns. Children cut and paste pictures on a worksheet to extend patterns *("Winter Wonders").*	Put a big picture of Santa and his sack on the bulletin board. Children cut out magazine pictures of toys to go into the sack and paste on the board. 	"Christmas Is Coming" "Elf Warm-up Exercises." Santa's elves must get in shape! Children touch toes, do sit-ups, run in place, do stretch-ups, and so on.	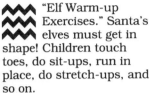 *ABC Christmas,* by Ida DeLage *Santa Claus Forever,* by Carolyn Haywood "The Little Elf," Hap Palmer, *Pretend*
THURSDAY	Discuss meaning of more, less, and equal. Ask children, Are there more girls or boys in our class? More tie shoes or velcro shoes? More blue eyes or brown? Let them figure out the answers.	Children string popcorn and cranberries using their own patterns. Less mature children can string Fruit Loops. 	Children make Santa from a star *("Santa Star Pattern").* They trace and cut out red stars, paste cotton balls on corners, and color a face and belt.	"We Wish You a Merry Christmas" "Up on the Housetop." Children play rhythm instruments, tapping out "click, click, click" to this popular song.	"A Merry-Mouse Christmas A-B-C," *A Merry-Mouse Treasury,* SVE *A Forest Christmas,* by Mayling Mack Holm *The Christmas Party,* by Adrienne Adams
FRIDAY	Have a Santa puppet ask children, What will you do this holiday? 	 Make *Christmas Cookies.* Children measure and mix ingredients. Cut into holiday shapes, decorate with *Egg Yolk Cookie Paint.*	Children make ornaments by painting pine cones and covering them with glue and glitter. 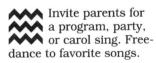	"Little Jack Horner" Invite parents for a program, party, or carol sing. Free-dance to favorite songs.	"Lollipop Dragon Helps Santa," *Holiday Adventures of the Lollipop Dragon,* SVE Santa visits! Have a party. 

JANUARY: WEEK 1
Let It Snow

	Thinking and Talking	Learning by Doing	Crafts and Creations	Songs and Games	Recommended Resources
MONDAY	Discuss weather. Show pictures of rain, snow, ice, fog, sun, and so on. Children describe weather, using the terms "sunny," "cloudy," "windy." Ask them if they prefer sunny days or rainy days. Why?	Give children a 1-to-1 correspondence worksheet and have them match hats to snowmen (*"Hats for Snowmen"*). 	Children make snow-people by pasting cotton on dark construction paper with 3 traced circles. Then they decorate using raisins for eyes, mouth, and buttons; a carrot piece for nose; and fabric strip for scarf.	"Here's a Hill" "Frosty the Snowman." One child puts on Frosty's hat. The rest follow movements as they dance around the room behind "Frosty."	 *Has Winter Come?* by Wendy Watson  "The Big Snow," Weston Woods *Tilabel,* by Patricia Coombs
TUESDAY	Have children sort pictures of weather activity scenes into seasons. How do we know it is winter? What are the signs of fall? How do we dress in the summer? What grows in the spring?	Bring clothes for all seasons to school: raincoat, umbrella, boots, swimsuit, shorts, sun hat, jacket, coat, scarf, mittens, sundress, sweatshirt, pants. Children take turns dressing up in winter clothes and summer clothes.	Children cut snowflakes from folded napkins or white paper (*"Snowflake Pattern"*).	"Snowflakes" "Pin the Nose on Frosty." Children use carrots made from construction paper.	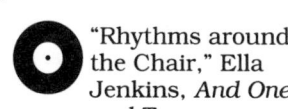 "Rhythms around the Chair," Ella Jenkins, *And One and Two* 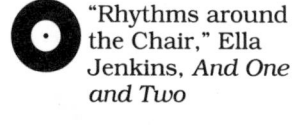 *The Snowy Day,* by Jack Ezra Keats 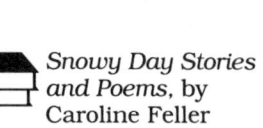 *Snowy Day Stories and Poems,* by Caroline Feller Bauer

Children play the "opposite game." Teacher says or shows a word, and children say or show opposite:
- hot—cold
- up—down
- tall—short

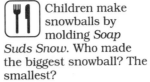 Make *Snow Cones.*

Children make snowballs by molding *Soap Suds Snow.* Who made the biggest snowball? The smallest?

 "Snowmen"

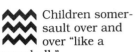 Children somersault over and over "like a snowball."

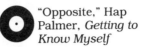 *Katy and the Big Snow,* by Virginia Lee Burton

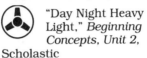 *The Tomten,* by Astrid Lindgren

"Opposite," Hap Palmer, *Getting to Know Myself*

"Day Night Heavy Light," *Beginning Concepts, Unit 2,* Scholastic

Draw a picture list as children brainstorm things to do in winter: build a snowman, ice skate, wear mittens, snow ski, sled, make snowballs, wear coats, and so on.

Have children melt ice cubes in their hand. Why did it turn to water? Put ice cubes in sun. What will happen? What happens if we put the melted water back in the freezer? Put water in a cup and mark the water line. Did it get bigger when it froze?

Children draw snow-scene pictures, using white chalk on black construction paper.

 "Five Little Snowmen"

 Play "Pass the Ice Cube" to music.

"I Saw Three Ships"

 *A January Fog Will Freeze a Hog,* by Hubert Davis

Go outside and build a snow figure or go sledding.

 Look at the thermometer each day and help children make a *Weather Chart* for the week: include temperature and 2 or 3 adjectives to describe conditions.

Mark a long zipper with thermometer readings and hang by calendar. During "opening circle" children take turns zipping it to the day's temperature.

Using balance scale, weigh and compare seasonal clothing. Which will weigh more, the hat or the mittens? The swimsuit or the jacket?

Using *Snow Paint,* paint a snow person on dark construction paper. When dry, color in eyes, nose, mouth, hat, arms with felt-tip pens.

 "Did You Ever See a Lassie"

 "The North Wind Doth Blow"

 Children pretend they are snow-flakes, drifting, dancing, and twirling to the ground. They lie on the floor and make "angels in the snow," moving arms and legs in and out.

 Snow, by Roy McKie and P. D. Eastman

 Have a skier visit and show his or her equipment.

 What Makes the Weather? by Janet Palazzo

 Winter, SVE

JANUARY: WEEK 2
Zip Up!

SKILLS TO INTRODUCE

- Describe weather using terms such as sunny, rainy, cold (S)
- Name and associate objects of clothing (SS)
- Follow directions (LA)
- Identify basic body parts (LA)
- Recognize absurdities in statements (LA)
- Manipulate laces, buttons, snaps, and zippers (LA)
- Sort and classify objects into sets (M)
- Demonstrate understanding of concepts of near and far, loud and soft, fast and slow, long and short, high and low (Mu)
- Paste paper and other materials to make collages (A)
- Create pictures, using paints (A)
- Demonstrate ability to change directions and go around obstacles while running (PE)
- Perform jumping tasks (PE)

	Thinking and Talking	Learning by Doing	Crafts and Creations	Songs and Games	Recommended Resources
MONDAY	 Show flannelboard pictures of different articles of clothing *("Winter Clothes and Summer Clothes")*. Children identify when we wear these clothes. Which do we wear when it rains? When it's sunny?	Bring a variety of clothes to school. Have children sort clothes by season, by body part, with and without buttons, and so on. Give children 2-to-3-step directions to put clothes away: "Put the mittens in the shoe box, the boots beside the front door, and sit in your chair."	Make *Banana Coconut Snowmen.* 	"Warm Hands" 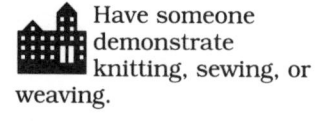 "Mulberry Bush"	*On the Town,* by Betsy Maestro *Peter's Pocket,* by Judi Barrett Have someone demonstrate knitting, sewing, or weaving.
TUESDAY	Put many pictures of clothing on floor. Ask each child to find a picture of something we wear on our feet or head or hands. Put out scarves of various lengths. Which is the longest? Shortest? Children place in order from longest to shortest.	Children practice manipulating laces, buttons, and so on with own clothes, dressing frames, dolls.  Give children a cardboard shoe to lace, *("Lacing Shoe Pattern")*. More mature students may attempt tying.	Make wall mural of winter scene. Have children paint snow, trees, snow people with *Snow Paint.*	"My Tall Silk Hat" "Cobbler, Cobbler"  Children put on big boots, carry umbrellas, and pretend they are playing in the rain. Teacher puts paper puddles on the floor. Children jump from puddle to puddle.	"Pick a Pattern, Pick a Patch," *People Who Work,* Unit 1, Scholastic *Max's New Suit,* by Rosemary Wells *New Clothes: What People Wore from Cavemen to Astronauts,* by Lisl Weil

WEDNESDAY

Does everyone around the globe wear the same clothes? Why not? Show pictures of children from different countries with different customs and weather. Discuss differences between their clothes and ours.

Children cut out pictures of clothes from a catalogue and hang them on a clothesline with clothespins.

Children make collages from dyed macaroni, rolled aluminum foil, buttons, fabric scraps, and so on.

 "Sleepy Fingers"

 "Fingers, Fingers, Everywhere"

 "The Three-cornered Hat"

 "What Are You Wearing?" Hap Palmer, *Learning Basic Skills Through Music, Vol. I*

 We Can Jump, by Barbara Williams

 The Mitten, by Alvin Tresselt

THURSDAY

Teacher makes statements, true and absurd; for example, "To go swimming, I wear my mittens," "If it is cold out, I need a hat." Children identify each as true or absurd.

Children put all their shoes in a pile in center of circle. They take turns finding a pair (not theirs) and returning to owner. (Can also be done with socks, mittens, etc.)

 Children cut along outline of mittens, *("Mittens")* and color and string them together. They write their name on each mitten.

 "Three Little Kittens"

 Children "skate" around the room to music. Have them skate slowly and skate quickly and freeze when the music stops.

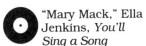 "Mary Mack," Ella Jenkins, *You'll Sing a Song*

Visit a shoe shop, a laundromat, a dress store.

 "Spider on the Floor," Raffi, *Singable Songs for the Very Young*

FRIDAY

Discuss different materials clothes are made from. Where do these materials come from?

Have "inside-out day." Send parents a note, telling them about the day. Children wear clothes inside-out, or backwards.

Trace around each child's shoe onto paper. Children color to resemble own shoe and cut out. Who has the biggest shoe? The smallest? The same size?

Have children bring an old T-shirt to school. With fabric flowpens or permanent magic markers, decorate!

 "Four Seasons"

 Set up a "dressing course." Children run to table and put on sweater, run to chair and put on boots, run to bathroom for a scarf, under a table for a hat, climb a ladder for a coat, and then go outside!

Have visitors wearing clothes from other countries.

Joseph's Other Red Sock, by Niki Daly

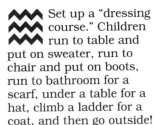 *Animals Should Definitely Not Wear Clothing*, by Judith Barrett

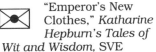 "Emperor's New Clothes," *Katharine Hepburn's Tales of Wit and Wisdom*, SVE

JANUARY: WEEK 3
Hickory Dickory Dock

SKILLS TO INTRODUCE

- Name some elements that make up our universe (S)
- Identify methods for measuring time (S)
- Tell a simple story (LA)
- Sequence events from a story (LA)
- Identify rhyming words (LA)
- Count by rote (M)
- Identify top, middle, and bottom of objects (M)
- Count up to 10 objects (M)
- Explore and create with rhythmic instruments (Mu)
- Use various mediums to print (A)
- Demonstrate ability in ball-handling skills (PE)

	Thinking and Talking	Learning by Doing	Crafts and Creations	Songs and Games	Recommended Resources
MONDAY	Show objects used to tell time: clocks, watches, calendar. Count numbers on them. Ask questions: which one tells us the hour? the day? where is the top of the calendar? 	Give children a paper with a sun at the top of one side and a moon at the other *("Daytime-Nighttime")*. Children draw "something we do at night" under moon and "something we do in the daytime" under sun.	Make sundials. On a sunny day, children go outside and stick pencil through paper plate in ground. Have them mark shadow of pencil every hour.	"Hey Diddle, Diddle" Give the children rubber balls. Have them count how many times they can bounce the ball before they miss. Have them bounce and recite: 1, 2, 3, Oh-Lary-oh 4, 5, 6, Oh-Lary-oh 7, 8, 9, Oh-Lary-oh and raise their leg over the ball on each *oh*.	*Tick Tick Clock*, by Sharon Gordon *What Time Is It?* by Judith Grey and Susan Hall "Slow Fast First Last," *Beginning Concepts, Unit 2*, Scholastic
TUESDAY	Using feltboard, show big clock and mouse *("Clock and Mouse Pattern")*. Say rhyme "Hickory Dickory Dock." Ask children where mouse is—bottom, middle, top. Ask children in turn to put mouse on bottom, middle, top.	Play rhyming game. Teacher says, "I'm thinking of a word that is the name of an animal and sounds like *house*." Answer: mouse. Rhyme with *moon*: spoon, tune, soon, balloon. Rhyme with *sun*: fun, run, bun, none.	Make walnut-shell mice with felt ears, commercial wiggle eyes, and yarn tail. Count how many. Line them up. 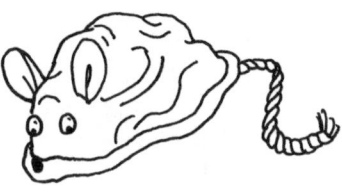	"Hickory Dickory Dock" Have children toss a velcro ball at a flannel clock and see who lands on the biggest number.	*All Year Long*, by Richard Scarry "Count, See, One, Two, Three," *Beginning Concepts, Unit 1*, Scholastic *Over and Over*, by Charlotte Zolotow

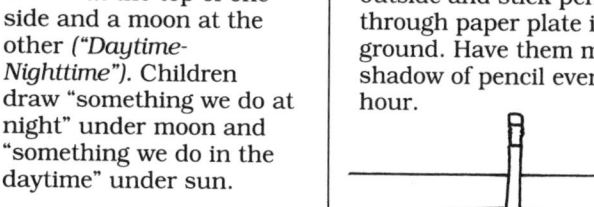

W E D N E S D A Y	Discuss today, yesterday, and tomorrow. Have students talk about what they did yesterday, what they will do tomorrow. Have them say the days of the week and months of the year in unison. Say them in a "giant" voice and in a "tiny mouse" voice.	Children put pictures of day activities in order. What do we do first, second? What do we do at 8:00 in the morning? Ask children each to tell a story about themselves—what did you do? "Once there was a little boy . . ."	Children make watches with cardboard face and felt wristband. They make face on watch. Glue velcro strips to fasten to their wrist.	"Chickamy, Craney, Crow" 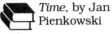 "Lazy Mary, Will You Get Up." Have children pretend to be asleep and then wake up when they hear this song. Set a timer, and children rise when it rings.	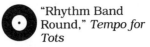 "Rhythm Band Round," *Tempo for Tots* 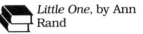 *Time*, by Jan Pienkowski *Little One*, by Ann Rand

T H U R S D A Y	Discuss day and night, sun and moon, activities for daytime and for nighttime. Show pictures of activities. Are these daytime or nighttime activities? 	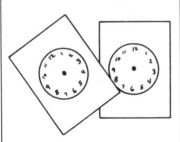 Children play lotto with paper clocks *("Clock Lotto").* Match clocks that have the same time.	Children make a paper-plate clock using a brad to attach the hands. Have them count the hours on the clock. 	"Noble Duke of York"  Have children use sticks and block instruments as they chant this song. Tell them to do it fast, slow. Have them pretend they are clocks and rock back and forth, clicking sticks and blocks to make a tick-tock sound. Set a timer and have children shake and shimmy as it rings.	"This Old Man" and "Hey What Country Folks We Be," Alan Mills, *14 Numbers, Letters, and Animal Songs*  "Paper Clocks," Hap Palmer, *Learning Basic Skills Through Music, Vol. II* *When? Pictures to Talk About*, by Leo Lionni

F R I D A Y	Talk about different seasons. In which season do we swim? skate? rake leaves? plant flowers? Have children say the seasons aloud in unison.	Make *Hot Choco-late*. Time kettle to see how many minutes to boiling. Serve each cup with 10 marshmallows for snack. Children count marshmallows. 	Children make potato print pictures of suns and moons with tempera on paper.	"Clocks" "Sing a Song of Six Pence." Point out rhyming words. 	*1 Is One*, by Tasha Tudor *Willy O'Dwyer Jumped in the Fire*, by Beatrice De Regniers 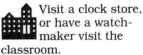 Visit a clock store, or have a watch-maker visit the classroom.

JANUARY: WEEK 4
Knock! Knock!

Carol's Bootery · BARGAINS · EVERYTHING REDUCED · OFFICE SUPPLIES

	Thinking and Talking	Learning by Doing	Crafts and Creations	Songs and Games	Recommended Resources
MONDAY	Discuss what a community is. A neighborhood? A city? A country? What places exist in a community (stores, banks, churches, schools, etc.)? Ask children where they are from. From this community? From this city?	Take a walk through community. Read signs for children. Have them guess by pictures and contents of store windows what purpose each building serves. On return to classroom, children draw their favorite building with crayons. Write name of building on each child's paper.	Make a big wall mural of stores. Have children cut out fabric shapes for different stores and color trees, sun, and grass.	"Knock at the Door" "London Bridge" "Little Mouse"	"Hansel and Gretel," DLM Developmental Storybooks "A Neighborhood Is a Friendly Place," Ella Jenkins, *Growing Up with Ella Jenkins* *Little Chestnut Tree Story*, by Lisl Weil
TUESDAY	Show children a map of their community. Point out well-known places, such as a park, fire station, school. Make a map of your classroom. 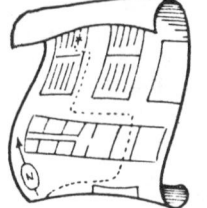	Play "Address Knock-Knock." Children chant "Knock, knock, who's there? Knock, knock, who's there? Knock, knock, who's there? Who is there this morning?" Child in center gives full name and then answers these questions asked by the class. • Where do you live? • In what country do you live? • How old are you?	Children paint with glue onto construction paper to form outline of a house. With brush and glue, they paint a door, windows, and chimney. Sprinkle with coffee grounds or cornmeal. 	"This Is the Church" Have children pretend their chair is a house. Have them follow commands: stand beside the house, behind the house, in front of the house, on top of, near, far from the house.	"People Packages," *Kindle I*, Scholastic *Deep in the Forest*, by Brinton Turkle *Boxes*, by M. Jean Craig

Show pictures of objects and ask where they might be found: bread, typewriter, scissors and comb, tire, dog, and so on. Children name buildings found in the city: bakery, office, barber shop, garage, pet store, and so on.

 Make *Parlor Pack Ice Cream.* Set up an ice cream parlor. To group children, label chairs with numbers. Children sit with others whose chairs have the same number.

 Children finger-paint using *fingerpaint* the color of their home. They use one finger to draw a house in the paint. Write address on bottom of picture as child dictates.

 "Finger Band"

 Put out instruments and have a "music store." Have children find instruments that are loud, soft, high, low. Have them demonstrate "fast" and "slow."

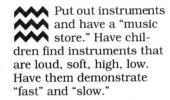 *The Night Flight,* by Joanne Ryder

 "Together" and "Yah-a-tay," *5 Families,* Scholastic

 Familar Sounds (tape), Developmental Learning Materials

Play a tape of sounds in the community and have children identify the sounds. Take a walk. What sounds do you hear?

Using snap-together blocks, Lincoln Logs, and other materials, children construct buildings. Take a photo of each child's construction, frame, and send home.

Children use wood scraps, glue, nails, and hammers to create the building of their choice— with adult supervision. Children can paint finished product with tempera paints.

 "Home on the Range"

Challenge the children to make buildings with their bodies and then line up the buildings in a row to make a street.

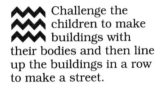 The Shopping Bag Lady, by Robert Censoni

 The Little House, by Virginia Lee Burton

Visit a house under construction, an office, or a factory.

Discuss buildings and objects found in the country and those found in a city. Do we see tractors in the city? Do we see auditoriums in the country? Do people live near each other in the city? In the country?

Write numerals on clip clothespins. Draw people inside shoebox houses. Children count number of people in house and clip on the corresponding clothespin.

Make a community. Put all Thursday's buildings on a big board. Have children paint roads and make grass with tissue paper, and telephone poles and wires with clothespins, clay, and yarn. Help them put up signs outside stores.

 "The House"

 Children act out story of "Hansel and Gretel."

 *Wake Up, City,* by Alvin Tresselt

Have a police officer visit the classroom. Children can share their name, address, and phone number.

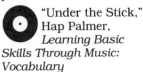 "Under the Stick," Hap Palmer, *Learning Basic Skills Through Music: Vocabulary*

FEBRUARY: WEEK 1
Rub-a-Dub-Dub

Rub - a - Dub - Dub

	Thinking and Talking	Learning by Doing	Crafts and Creations	Songs and Games	Recommended Resources
MONDAY	Bring in or collect from parents different career hats. Put them on one by one and ask children to tell you what your job is. Where does this person work?	Tape sheets of paper over pictures of different workers and cut paper away little by little until children can guess who they are. 	Help children make *candles.*	"Police Officer"  "Mulberry Bush"	*What Do People Do All Day?* by Richard Scarry "Bake a Batch of Bread," *People Who Work, Unit 1,* Scholastic "I'm a Policeman," *Disney's Children's Favorites, Vol. 1*
TUESDAY	Which people in the community help us keep healthy? safe? build? get food? Look at the yellow pages of telephone book together.	Give children different duties in classroom. Make a "helping hands" chart. Rotate throughout rest of year. Collect food containers and set up a "supermarket" with stock clerk, cashier, delivery people and so on.	Children make badges covered with aluminum foil. They can pretend to be police officers, fire chiefs, and so on. Give commands of 2 to 3 steps for children to imitate based on their job.	"Ten Brave Firefighters" "Police Officer Freeze." One child is police officer. Rest of children move around room. When police officer blows whistle, they halt.	*Who's Got the Apple?* by Jan Loof  "I Want to Be a Farmer," Nancy Raven, *Hop, Skip and Sing* *Martin's Hat,* by Joan Blos 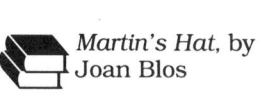

WEDNESDAY

Some people have more than one job. Do mothers and fathers have more than one job? There are jobs that we get paid for and jobs we do for free. Do you do any jobs at home? Why do we do these jobs?

 Set up a restaurant. Children make and serve *Individual Pizzas*. They also practice clean-up skills such as wiping tables and washing dishes.

 Children make tissue-paper chef's hats (*"Chef's Hat"*).

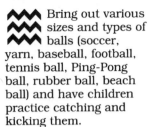

 "Ten Workers"

 Bring out various sizes and types of balls (soccer, yarn, baseball, football, tennis ball, Ping-Pong ball, rubber ball, beach ball) and have children practice catching and kicking them.

 Six Foolish Fisherman, by Benjamin Elkin

Visit a police station, a bakery, a butcher shop, or a factory.

Piro and the Fire Brigade, by Kurt Baumann

THURSDAY

Name a profession and ask children to tell you what a person has to learn to perform that particular job. Where or how does one learn these things?

Have several sacks with pictures of workers pasted on the front. Have children sort "tools" and items into proper sacks: hammer—carpenter, scissors—beautician, frying pan—chef, books—teacher.

On cardboard pizza circles, children create "pizzas" by painting red tomato sauce and shaking cornmeal (grated cheese) on top. Carrots dipped in tempera can be used to print pepperoni slices or black olives, and mushrooms can be used to print mushrooms.

 "Jack, Be Nimble"

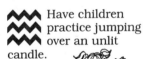 Have children practice jumping over an unlit candle.

 Invite parents to talk about their work.

 "Bumping Up and Down," Raffi, *Singable Songs for the Very Young*

 *I'm a Big Helper*, by Sylvia Tester

FRIDAY

What job would you like to have when you are older? Why? Children take turns being "foreman" giving directions to the other "workers" such as "saw that wood," "hammer those nails," "unscrew those screws." Class role plays these directions.

 Give children a 1-to-1 correspondence worksheet (*"Workers and Tools"*). Have them match workers to tools. Encourage left-to-right, top-to-bottom orientation.

Children draw picture of themselves when they are grown up, performing their dream job. Frame with construction paper.

 "Rub-a-Dub-Dub"

"The Muffin Man"

 What Do They Do? by Carla Greene

"I Got a Job," Ella Jenkins, *Growing Up with Ella Jenkins*

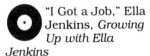 "Let's Guess: What Person Is It?" *What Is It?* Encyclopedia Britannica

FEBRUARY: WEEK 2
Sealed with a Kiss

Be Mine

	Thinking and Talking	Learning by Doing	Crafts and Creations	Songs and Games	Recommended Resources
MONDAY	Discuss these questions: What is love? Who do you love? Who loves you? What different ways are there to show a person you love them? What are nice "words" to say to someone special?	Children make *Strawberry Milkshakes*. Pass out straws. Children can find a partner, sit together, and share a milkshake. 	Children fold paper in half, draw an arc, cut on line, and open for a Valentine. Then they color, decorate with glitter, write their name inside, and give it to their mom or dad.	"Five Little Valentines" Have a Valentine's tug-of-war, with girls against boys. 	*Valentine's Day Grump,* by Rose Greydanus "Hey, We'll Fill the World with Love," Rosenshontz, *Tickles You!* Visit a post office or have a mail carrier visit the classroom.
TUESDAY	Communications: What are different ways to let people know of things that happen: talking, telephone, letters, telegrams, telex, television, radio, newspapers. Show examples or pictures of these. 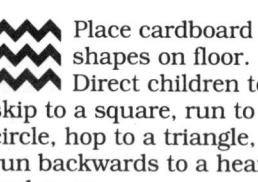	Make classroom post office by gluing together shoe boxes that the children have decorated. Have children write their first name on small cards. Paste one card on each box.	Children make Valentines for each other. Give children heart stencils of different sizes to trace, doilies, ribbons, glitter, construction paper, and so on. Let them create. Put Valentines in post boxes.	"Valentine's Good Morning" "Love Somebody" 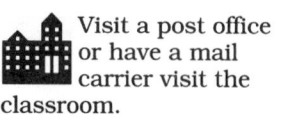 Place cardboard shapes on floor. Direct children to skip to a square, run to a circle, hop to a triangle, run backwards to a heart, and so on.	*Arthur's Valentine,* by Marc Brown Visit a radio or television station or a newspaper office. *The Valentine's Bears,* by Eve Bunting

WEDNESDAY

Talk about different careers in communications, from mail carrier to TV producer.

Cut out cardboard box bottom or side to resemble TV screen. Have children take turns sitting behind screen to tell an important news item or to perform.

Create classroom newspaper. Each child draws small picture about an important event and dictates a sentence or two about it, which teacher writes down. All pictures are pasted on both sides of big white paper to make the newspaper.

  "Valentine"

 "I Love You"

 "Will You Be My Valentine?"

 "The Mail Must Go Through," *Disney's Children's Favorites, Vol. 1*

 "Sara's Letter," *5 Children*, Scholas- tic

One Zillion Valentines, by Frank Modell

THURSDAY

Discuss Lincoln's and Washington's birthdays. What is a president? What does he do? Who is our president now? Give children simple historical background on Lincoln and Washington.

 Give children an outline of Lincoln's head, *("Abraham Lincoln")*. They tear small pieces of black construction paper to make a mosaic silhouette.

Children make cherry trees. They draw and color green tree, and cut out small red construction paper circles and paste on tree for cherries.

 Act out "cherry tree" story with children. Discuss the importance of telling the truth.

 "Paper of Pins"

 "Won't You Be My Friend," Hap Palmer, *Getting to Know Myself*

Bee My Valentine, by Miriam Cohen

Valentine Day, by Judith Hoffman Conwin

FRIDAY

Show and name different shapes. Which shape is associated with Valentine's Day? Why? What colors?

Children string pasta that has been tinted red, white, and pink onto yarn with taped tip to make a Valentine necklace. (Dye pasta with food color and rubbing alcohol.)

Children make Valentine hearts by pasting a red square and 2 half circles together. With a heart-shaped sponge dipped in paint, they print hearts around the edge.

 Have a Valentine's party. Ask parents to provide a heart-shaped treat. Everyone wears something red or pink! Free-dance to music with a friend.

 "Polly Wolly Doodle"

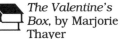 "Lollipop Dragon's Valentine's Party," *Holiday Adventures of the Lollipop Dragon*, SVE

The Valentine's Box, by Marjorie Thayer

FEBRUARY: WEEK 3
Our Growing Bodies

	Thinking and Talking	Learning by Doing	Crafts and Creations	Songs and Games	Recommended Resources
MONDAY	How do we know if an object is alive or not alive? What do things need to stay alive? Discuss such answers as oxygen, carbon dioxide, food, water, sunlight.	Show pictures of living and nonliving things *(Living and Nonliving Things)*. Have children distinguish and categorize. 	Divide each child's paper in 4 parts. Have them draw and color different stages of life in each box: baby, child, young adult, old adult.	"Dentist"  "Skip to My Lou"	*You Can't Move Without Your Muscles*, by Paul Showers "A Healthy Day," *Slim Goodbody's Health Series*, SVE 
TUESDAY	Discuss things we can do to make our bodies healthy. Discuss body parts and their functions: eyes—see, ears—hear, nose—smell, hair—warmth, stomach—digestion, feet—movement, and so on.	Give each child a toothbrush. Demonstrate correct way to brush. Talk about when to brush and why. Have children brush teeth after snack or lunch. 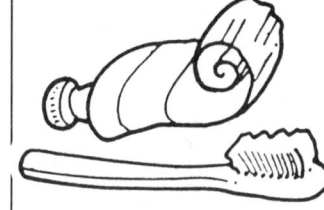	Children make watermelons from a half-circle cut from red construction paper. They color the rind, and paste on seeds. Have them count how many. 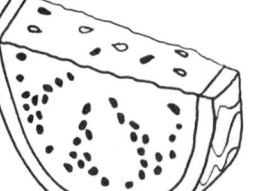	"Wee Willie Winkie" Play soft music as children relax on floor. Direct them to slowly move body parts: "Slowly raise your arm to the sky; Slowly lift your head, and release. Open and close your legs."	*Learning Basic Skills Through Music: Health and Safety*, Hap Palmer "Say Ah," *People Who Work, Unit 1*, Scholastic *My Friend the Doctor*, by Jane Werner Watson

WEDNESDAY

Which professionals help us to stay healthy? Discuss the work of doctors, dentists, nurses, hygienists.

Give children red construction paper to cut out smiling lips. They then cut strips of white paper into "teeth" and glue between the smiling lips. (White beans can also be used.)

Children paint pictures with old toothbrushes.

 "Good Night"

 "Ten in the Bed"

 "Something About Me"

 The Tooth Fairy, by Sharon Peters

 The Bear's Toothache, by David McPhail

 "Brush Your Teeth," Raffi, *Singable Songs for the Very Young*

THURSDAY

Make a chart, "Things I Do to Be Healthy." Have children check off items each day. The chart could include brushing teeth, eating a good breakfast, wearing appropriate clothes.

Show pictures of items that help keep us healthy, such as soap, sun, carrot, toothbrush. Children tell how each one helps us. Children draw a healthy meal or snack on a paper plate.

Children make stethoscopes with pipe cleaners and an empty spool or bottle cap.

 Set up a fitness test that includes running forward and backward, jumping over a stick, balancing on 1 foot, walking sideways, hopping on each foot, touching toes.

 "Two Little Hands So Clean and Bright"

 What's Good for a Four-Year-Old, by William Cole

 My Friend the Dentist, by Jane Werner Watson

FRIDAY

Measure and weigh children. Compare figures with those of September, Week 2. Compare different heights and weights of children. Line children up from shortest to tallest. Make bar graph.

If possible borrow a skeleton from a high school or college and set up in classroom. String macaroni to look like a backbone. Have children hold them up so they are straight and healthy, or let them sag so they demonstrate poor posture.

 Help children prepare a *Fresh Fruit Salad*.

 "'To Bed! To Bed!' Says Sleepy Head"

 Play 3 styles of music. Have children identify which songs are classical, western, and rock. Children can move freely to the beat of the music.

 Visit a doctor, nurse, or dentist, or have one visit the classroom.

 *Curious George Goes to the Hospital*, by H. A. Rey

 My Dentist, Harlow Rockwell

"Kitten Pup Grows Up," *Beginning Concepts, Unit 2*, Scholastic

FEBRUARY: WEEK 4
Better Watch Out!

SKILLS TO INTRODUCE

- Identify emotions and feelings (SS)
- Match common objects found in the home to appropriate location (SS)
- Give reasons why people work (SS)
- Give examples and reasons for school and community rules (SS)
- Comprehend and follow basic safety rules (SS)
- Say first and last name (LA)
- Recite address and phone number (LA)
- Sequence events from a story (LA)
- Identify ordinals: first, second, third, and last (M)
- Create pictures with paints (A)
- Manipulate hands correctly for fingerplays (Mu)
- Participate successfully in games and organized activities (PE)

	Thinking and Talking	Learning by Doing	Crafts and Creations	Songs and Games	Recommended Resources
MONDAY	Discuss ways we can keep safe. Who helps us keep safe? (parents, police, firefighters) One child puts on a police hat and plays police officer, asking children their name and phone number. 	✏️ Children cut and paste patterns onto popsicle sticks to make traffic signs (*"Safety Signs"*).	Using stencil shaped like a stop sign, children take turns easel painting a red stop sign. Help each child write "STOP" with black markers when dry.	✿ "Stop, Look, and Listen" 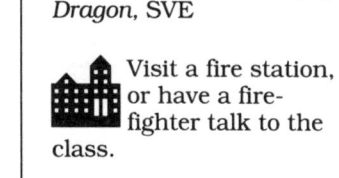 ♪ "Shoo Fly"	📚 *Make Way for Ducklings,* by Robert McCloskey ☉ "Remembering and Using Safety Rules," *Safety Adventures of the Lollipop Dragon,* SVE 🏢 Visit a fire station, or have a firefighter talk to the class.
TUESDAY	Show pictures of safety signs. Have children identify what each means.  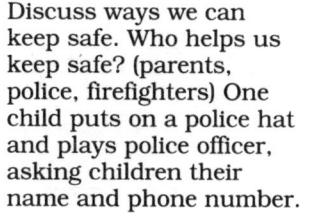	Write down each child's telephone number. Have them each practice dialing their number (and push-buttoning it). Give each child your telephone number. Have them call you from home in the evening as practice. 	Have children cut out magazine pictures of things that shouldn't be touched by children without adult supervision: matches, cleaning fluids and detergents, knives, medicines, and so on. Paste onto paper.	✌ "Traffic Lights"  ❋ "Red Light, Green Light." Children run toward leader, but must freeze when leader says, "Red light" and turns to face children. If leader sees child move, child must return to "go." The winner becomes the next leader.	📚 *Never Talk to a Stranger,* by Irma Joyce ◉ "Red Light, Green Light," *Tempo for Tots* 🏢 Have a police officer visit.

WEDNESDAY	What school rules do we have? Why? What rules do you have at home? Do they help you keep safe? What is a fire drill?	Small groups play board games that have rules, such as Candyland, Chutes and Ladders, Color Bingo, Lotto. Talk about why these rules are important.	Cooking without cooking: *No-Bake Yummies.*	"Firefighter" "Follow the Police Officer." One child wears a police officer's hat and the others follow, walking, skipping, hopping, "across the street."	*All Kinds of Signs,* by Seymour Reit *Too Smart for Strangers,* Walt Disney *Firefighters,* by Nancy Robinson

THURSDAY	Talk about "stranger danger." How should a child act? What should you do first? second? third? Run, and tell your parents or another adult.
	 Use a "stranger danger" puppet who tries to trick a child. "Come, little one, get into my car, and I'll take you to your mommy." What should the "smart child" puppet reply?
		Read *Little Red Riding Hood* using flannelboard figures. (If flannel figures aren't available, cut pictures from a book and glue felt strips on the back.) Have children take turns reciting the story in proper order. What did the wolf do first? What is the lesson to be learned from this story?	Children take turns reciting their address and phone number. Make safety bracelets. On strip of paper, write child's name and phone number. Child decorates other side. Attach with clear adhesive tape.	"Looby Loo"
				
				  Set up a "road" with stop signs. Children take turns riding a tricycle, stopping at each sign. 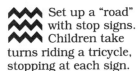
					Mushroom in the Rain, by Mirra Ginsburg
					
					 Poisons Make You Sick, by Dorothy Chlad
					
					  "I'm a Policeman Dressed in Blue," *Disney's Children's Favorites, Vol. 1*

FRIDAY	Talk about feeling scared, feeling safe. What things make you feel these ways? 	Discuss safety in home. Show pictures of objects in wrong places where they might cause harm; for example, knife on floor, ball on stairs. Ask children where these things should be kept for safety. 	Children make "fire pictures" with red and yellow *fingerpaints.*	"Safety Belts"  "Flashlight Tag." Turn out the lights and have the children play tag with a flashlight.	*Matches and Fireworks Are Not Toys,* by Dorothy Chlad  "Safety Signs," Hap Palmer, *Learning Basic Skills Through Music: Vocabulary* "Stop, Look, Listen," "Safe Way," and "Buckle Your Seat Belt," Hap Palmer, *Learning Basic Skills Through Music: Health and Safety*

MARCH: WEEK 1
Here Comes the Circus

	Thinking and Talking	Learning by Doing	Crafts and Creations	Songs and Games	Recommended Resources
MONDAY	Show pictures of animals. Ask children to identify which ones they might find in a circus. 	Give children the worksheet *"Elephant Parade."* Tell them to color the blanket of the first one blue, the second one pink, the third one red, the last one yellow. Then the remainder of the picture can be colored as children desire.	Help children make cone-shaped clown hats out of construction paper. Have children decorate with cut-out shapes, stickers, tissue paper, crepe paper. Staple on elastic chin strap. 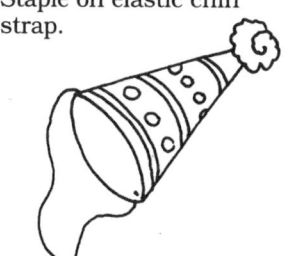	"Five Little Clowns" 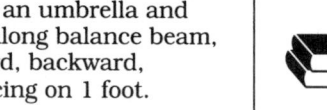 "Yankee Doodle"	*Dandy's Dandy Lions,* by Bill Pett "Circus Family," 5 *Families,* Scholastic *The Circus Baby,* by Maud Petersham
TUESDAY	Play a tape of animal sounds. Children listen to them and identify. Which animal is the favorite? Graph replies.	Be silly clowns. Make statements about circus characters and have children act out the opposite. When you say, "The clown was sitting down," the children stand up. 	Cut holes in shoe boxes to imitate cages. Have children cut out and paste magazine pictures of animals in each "cage." 	"Eenie, Meenie, Minie, Moe" Children pretend to be tightrope walkers and carry an umbrella and walk along balance beam, forward, backward, balancing on 1 foot.	*Bear Circus,* by William DuBois "The Clown," Hap Palmer, *Pretend* *Mishka,* by Victor Ambrus

WEDNESDAY

 Using feltboard and circus figures *("Circus Patterns"),* ask children to place ball next to clown, on top of clown, and so on. Then position pictures and ask, "Where is the ball?" Response: "Under the clown."

Hide peanuts in the classroom. Children become elephants and hunt for hidden peanuts. They can tell where they found them—inside the dollhouse, under the sandtable, behind the piano.

Children use fingers to print, and add details with pens to make fingerprints into circus animals.
  Make a circus train of elephants, walking behind one another.

 "This Little Clown"

 "One Little Elephant"

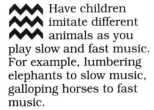 Have children imitate different animals as you play slow and fast music. For example, lumbering elephants to slow music, galloping horses to fast music.

 Clowns, by Harriet Langsamsobol

 "Tightrope Walker," *Preschool Fitness*

 Jacko, by John S. Goodall

THURSDAY

Review shapes and colors. Play "Pass the Shape." When music stops, have each child tell which shape he or she is holding. "I have a red square." "I have a yellow circle."

Have children classify opposites. Make two big rings on floor. Tell children to put small stuffed animals in one ring, large ones in other. Next, classify by dark and light, then fierce and tame.

 Make *Circus Popcorn.*

 Children make "wheelbarrows" with a partner. One child walks on hands while partner holds feet.

 "Here Sits a Monkey"

 "High-wire Artist," Hap Palmer, *Easy Does It*

 Circus, by Beatrice Schenk De Regiers

 Go to a circus.

FRIDAY

Talk about feelings that a circus evokes. Can it be funny? sad? scary? Draw happy, sad, scared faces on balloons.

 Give children a picture of a clown *("Balloons for the Clown").* Have them draw and color balloons their favorite colors.

If you were a clown, how would you like to look: funny, scary, sad, angry? Children draw a clown face that depicts them as a clown.

 Using nontoxic *face paint,* paint children's faces to make them clowns. Let them go home painted.

 "Five Big Elephants"

 Have a circus. Children can pretend to be galloping horses, lion tamers, dancing bears, human cannonballs, tigers jumping through hoops, balancing elephants. Have children perform for parents or another class.

✉ *Dumbo,* Walt Disney

 Roncall's Magnificent Circus, by Gabriel Lisowski

Have a clown or a juggler visit the classroom.

MARCH: WEEK 2
Lucky Green Shamrocks

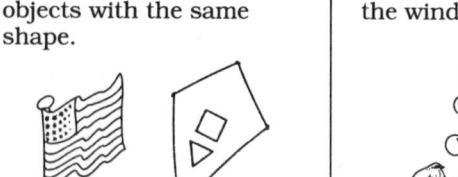

	Thinking and Talking	Learning by Doing	Crafts and Creations	Songs and Games	Recommended Resources
MONDAY	Talk about March weather: the wind. Ask children to name things the wind can blow: hats, scarves, flags, kites, sailboats, pinwheels, windmills, umbrellas, hair, clouds, trees. Can you see the wind?	Give children a shamrock with holes punched around the edge *("Shamrock Pattern")*. Have them string a piece of yarn, sewing around the holes.	Children color designs on flat coffee filters, using brightly colored felt markers. Dip in water and watch the colors blend. Hang with yarn from ceiling.	"The Wind" "I Am a Fine Musician" "Musical Chairs." Line up chairs, 1 less than number of children. Children march around chairs to music. When record stops, the child without chair is "out." Remove 1 chair each round.	*The North Wind and the Sun*, illus. by Brian Wildsmith Visit a science museum, or have a scientist visit and perform experiments with air. *Curious George Flies a Kite*, by Margaret Rey
TUESDAY	Bring objects that exemplify 2-D and 3-D shapes. Talk about uses. Have children name other objects with the same shape. 	Children make bubbles *(Bubble Solution)*. Blow them, watch them float in the wind. 	Children blow-paint pictures. Put spoonfuls of various colors of tempera in middle of paper. Children blow a design, using a straw.	"Buttercups and Daisies" "Blow." Divide class into 2 teams. Each tries to blow a Ping-Pong ball off table on opposing team's side. 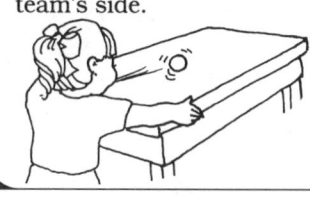	*The Wind Thief*, by Judy Barrett "The Kite Song," Hap Palmer, *Pretend* *The Wind Blew*, by Pat Hutchins

WEDNESDAY	Go outside and fly a kite, weather permitting. Talk about why kites go up, down, don't fly. Talk about what the tail is for. 	Children design, color, and cut out kite in any desired shape: circular, hexagonal, diamond. Have them make a tail with yarn and crushed tissue paper; attach to kite. Fill bulletin board with the kites.	Children make leprechauns out of paper bags. Put yarn in top for hair and tie shut with piece of yarn. Glue on construction paper feet. Make oval ears; draw circles for eyes, rectangle for nose, tiny squares for mouth. 	"A Kite" "Let's Go Fly a Kite." Fly a kite outside. Then children imitate kites, floating and whirling around.	*Where Does the Butterfly Go When It Rains?* by May Garelick "What Do You See? Color!" and "What Do You See? Shapes!" *Color, Shape, and Size,* Encyclopedia Britannica
THURSDAY	Talk about patterns. Have children point out patterns in the room, on clothes, walls. Demonstrate shape patterns on feltboard *(Lucky Charms)* Have volunteers copy and extend patterns.	Children make rainbows with colored chalk and identify colors used. They then draw a pot of gold at the end of the rainbow and write "rainbow names," using a different color for each letter. 	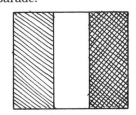 Children make *Irish Flags.* Emphasize left-to-right progression. Have children color first green, then white, then orange. Staple to straw and use in parade.	 "Leaves" "Beanbag-Shape Toss." Children try to throw beanbag onto various cardboard shapes on floor. How far can you throw? Identify colors and shapes.	"One Shape, Three Shapes" and "Triangle, Circle, and Square," Hap Palmer, *Learning Basic Skills Through Music, Vol. II* *The Hungry Leprechaun,* by Mary Calhoun
FRIDAY	Invite an Irish parent, teacher, or older student to come and share a story or song about St. Patrick's Day.	Make green *Gelatin Cubes.* Cut into shapes with cookie cutters. Have children predict the change from liquid to solid in the refrigerator.	 Children make shamrocks by cutting out 3 heart shapes and a stem and stapling or pasting together *("Three-Heart Shamrock").* Cover with small pieces of green tissue paper or cellophane.	"Mary Wore Her Red Dress" Have a St. Patrick's Day parade. Children march around with musical instruments to music. Everyone wears green!	*Little Bear Marches in the St. Patrick's Day Parade,* by Janice *St. Patrick's Day in the Morning,* by Eve Bunting *St. Patrick's Day,* SVE

MARCH: WEEK 3
Nuts for Nutrition

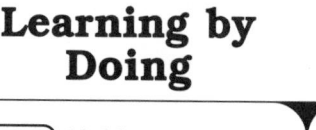

SKILLS TO INTRODUCE

- Distinguish between healthy and junk foods (S)
- Measure amounts of liquids and solids (S)
- Categorize common foods (S)
- Practice good health habits (S)
- Use comparative and superlative adjectives (LA)
- Follow maze and connect dot-to-dot patterns (LA)
- Compare sets to determine if they have more, less, or equal number of members (M)
- Sing class songs from memory (Mu)
- Paste paper and other materials to make collages (A)
- Perform climbing skills (PE)
- Demonstrate dynamic and static balance (PE)

	Thinking and Talking	Learning by Doing	Crafts and Creations	Songs and Games	Recommended Resources
MONDAY	Make a class chart of children's favorite foods after a group discussion on the subject. 	Children trace simple dot-to-dot patterns to make food pictures *("Dot-to-Dot Food")*. 	Children drizzle glue on a paper, making various designs. Sprinkle with cornmeal. 	"Here's a Cup of Tea" "I'm a Nut" 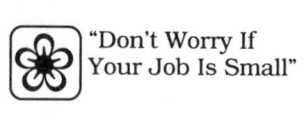	*Good for Me! All About Food in 32 Bites,* by Marilyn Burns Have lunch in a restaurant. 
TUESDAY	Discuss which foods help us grow and stay healthy and which don't. Name foods and have children cheer for good ones and boo for bad ones. 	Give children worksheet and have them draw in roads from food to source *("Follow the Path").* 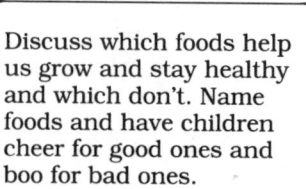	Children make a collage of various shells—peanut shells, walnut shells, egg shells, pecan shells.	"Mabel, Mabel" Children pretend they are elephants and stand on 1 foot and catch a peanut thrown by teacher. "Don't Worry If Your Job Is Small"	"Short, Tall, Large, Small," *Beginning Concepts, Unit 1,* Scholastic *On Top of Spaghetti,* by Tom Glazer "Ten Green Apples," by Ella Jenkins, *Growing Up with Ella Jenkins*

WEDNESDAY

Bring in an assortment of fruits, 3 of each kind. Show 2 and ask children to tell which is bigger, smaller. Show 3 and ask which is biggest, smallest. Set out several small baskets of mixed fruits. Which has the most, the least? Do any have the same number of pieces? Which one is empty?

Set out 16 cups of liquid, a pint container, a quart container, and a gallon container. Count together how many cups fill a pint, a quart, and a gallon. Which container holds the most, the least?

Children make tablecloths for Friday's luncheon by printing designs on big sheets of paper with fruits and vegetables.

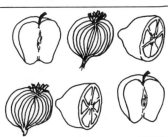

 "Paw-Paw Patch"

 Children take turns climbing a ladder to hang paper apples or oranges on a big tree on top of the bulletin board.

 Carrot Cake, by Nonny Hogrogian

Blueberries for Sal, by Robert McCloskey

Have a visitor cook an ethnic food for the class.

THURSDAY

Present children with a variety of dairy products, fruits, and vegetables, meats, and grains. Explain that there are 4 food groups. Have children categorize the foods into the proper groups.

Plan a luncheon. Draw foods you are going to cook.

 Ideas: *Celery Boats, Spaghetti and Meatballs, Garlic Bread, Apple Crisp.* Invite parents for luncheon.

Make a mobile on a coat hanger. Have children draw, color, and cut out one representative food from each food group. Secure foods on hanger with string. Hang in classroom.

 "Little Tom Tucker"

 "Peanut Butter"

 The Snacking Mouse" and "The Snacking Mouse Goes to School" and "Nutrition for Children," *Nutrition Filmstrip Series,* The Polished Apple

Popcorn, by Millicent Selsam

FRIDAY

Ask children to tell you which they like better, food A or food B. Have them ask their neighbor in circle the same question.

Divide children into groups to prepare foods for luncheon. Remind them to wash hands first. Discuss why these foods make us healthy. Point out various tools of measurement while cooking.

Children paint a still life of fruit. Have them paint with cotton balls instead of brushes. (For less mess, hold cotton ball with clothespin.)

 "Polly Put the Kettle On"

 "Peanut Race." Children push peanut across the floor with their nose and run back. Then they carry the peanut across the room on a spoon and hop back.

 "Toot! Toot!"

 *The Carrot Seed*, by Ruth Krauss

Bread and Jam for Frances, by Russell Hoban

 "Tree Fell Down," Hap Palmer, *Easy Does It*

MARCH: WEEK 4
Peter Cottontail

	Thinking and Talking	Learning by Doing	Crafts and Creations	Songs and Games	Recommended Resources
MONDAY	Introduce the word *Easter.* Have children give information they know about this holiday; you can add to this. Talk about Passover. Discuss holiday traditions. What special foods do we eat at Easter? At Passover? Who is the Easter Bunny? Will anyone special visit during the holidays?	It's Humpty Dumpty Day! Act out this nursery rhyme with the children. Make *Humpty Dumpty Eggs,* letting each child crack his or her own Humpty Dumpty. What happens to the liquid when we cook it?	Trace large Easter egg pattern on construction paper (*"Giant Easter Egg"*). Have children cut out, color designs on with crayon, and then paint over with diluted tempera so crayon shows through.	"Little Bunny Foo Foo" "Pin the Cottonball on the Bunny" 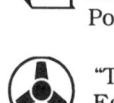	*The Tale of Peter Rabbit,* by Beatrix Potter "The Big Easter Egg Hunt," *Holiday Adventures of the Lollipop Dragon,* SVE "Silly Rabbit," *Preschool Fitness* *Green Eggs and Ham,* by Dr. Seuss
TUESDAY	Demonstrate different actions: running, walking, nodding, smiling, and so on. Have children name them. Then have children demonstrate an action and others name it. 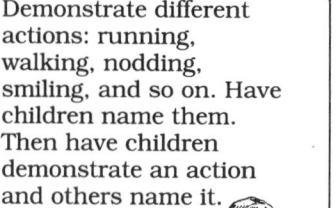	Give the children a worksheet with rows of Easter eggs outlined on it (*"Easter Eggs"*). See if they can finish each row, extending the pattern. 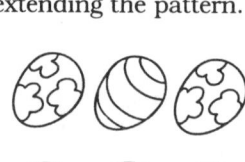	With clay, children make baskets and eggs to go in them. Tell children how many eggs to make for each basket to practice numbers 1 to 10.	"Five Little Easter Rabbits" "Little Peter Rabbit" 	*The Easter Bunny That Overslept,* by Priscilla Friedrich and Otto Friedrich *A Rabbit for Easter,* by Carol Carrick "The Rabbit Hop," *Tempo for Tots*

WEDNESDAY	Children rhyme with Easter words: An Easter *bunny* is very ___. He gave *Meg* a pretty colored ___. A-tisket, a-*tasket*, a green and yellow ___. Mother's going to *bake* a special Easter ___. I told the bunny to *stop, stop, stop*, but he only wanted to ___, ___, ___.	Make paper rabbits with numbers on their stomachs and cover with clear adhesive plastic *("Button Bunny").* Pass out rabbits to children and have them put as many buttons on stomach as shown by numeral. Pass rabbits to the left and repeat.	Help children draw outline of a rabbit. They can fill in outline with cotton and color ears pink. (Brown or white beans can also be used.) 	"Humpty Dumpty" Children have relays hopping like a bunny, rolling like an egg, skipping like a child.	*The Runaway Bunny,* by Margaret Wise Brown *Rackety: That Very Special Rabbit,* by Margaret Friskey *The Tale of Peter Rabbit,* Weston Woods 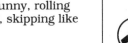 "All the Ways of Jumping," Hap Palmer, *Walter the Waltzing Worm*
THURSDAY	Play "Number Guessing Game." Say, "I'm thinking of a number that tells me how many ears a bunny has, . . . a number that tells me how many paws a rabbit has."	Set out baskets filled with straw or grass, clipping a number on the front of each basket. Children place appropriate number of plastic eggs in each basket.	Make bunny ears together. *("Bunny Headband").* Have a hopping race or a bunny hide-and-seek game. 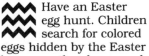	"Bunny" Children line up behind teacher, holding onto the waist of the child in front. Follow the teacher in the "Bunny Hop."	"6 Little Ducks," Alan Mills, *14 Numbers, Letters and Animal Songs* 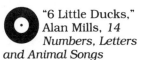 *The Egg Tree,* by Katherine Milhous Visit a hatchery, or set up a class-room incubator.
FRIDAY	Talk about eggs. Where do they come from? What is inside them? What animals lay eggs? Does an egg grow? Or does something grow inside it? 	Open up a raw egg and ask children to predict what will happen to eggs when cooked for a long time. Then boil eggs. Children decorate eggs for an Easter egg hunt, using food coloring, crayons, stickers, and sequins.	Children make Easter bonnets by gluing items such as dried and plastic flowers, buttons, bows, yarn pieces, sequins, and feathers onto a paper plate. Secure ribbon to plate and tie under each child's chin.	"Five Pretty Easter Eggs" Have an Easter egg hunt. Children search for colored eggs hidden by the Easter bunny on the playground or in classroom. Have an Easter party.	*Morning, Rabbit, Morning,* by Mary Caldwell *The Passover Parrot,* by Evelyn Zusman Invite a costumed bunny or "Big Bird" to visit. *Golden Egg Book,* by Margaret Wise Brown

APRIL: WEEK 1
Spring Has Sprung

SKILLS TO INTRODUCE

- Identify seasonal changes (S)
- Name necessary elements for plant growth (S)
- Identify basic parts of a plant (S)
- Identify whole picture when only part is shown (LA)
- Associate objects by given attributes (LA)
- Recognize numerals (M)
- Listen to music for enjoyment (Mu)
- Work with classmates on group art projects (A)
- Create pictures with paints (A)
- Participate successfully in games and organized activities (PE)
- Creep and crawl in various ways (PE)

	Thinking and Talking	Learning by Doing	Crafts and Creations	Songs and Games	Recommended Resources
MONDAY	Talk about parts of the plant, using a real plant as model. Stalk or stem, roots, ground—what is each part's function? 	Experiment: Place 2 white carnations, with stems split halfway up, into 2 jars of water with different food coloring solutions. Children will see how the color climbs up the flower.	Give each child an empty spool to paint. Then teacher paints a face and attaches a long string. Children string their spools together to make a very long classroom caterpillar.	"Grasshoppers" Pair children; one is "apple," the other is "caterpillar." Caterpillar crawls between legs of apple.	*The Very Hungry Caterpillar*, by Eric Carle Visit a florist or a greenhouse. Have someone demonstrate flower arranging. *Make Way for Ducklings*, by Robert McCloskey
TUESDAY	Bring in fruits and vegetables that have seeds inside. Ask children to guess what is the same about all of them. Open them and begin a discussion of seeds.	Make *Lentil Soup*. 	Children paste a small branch onto construction paper. (If unavailable, draw a branch.) Children glue small cotton balls or puffed rice along branch to make pussy willows. Count how many cotton balls. Trade with a friend and count cotton balls. Who used more?	"The Flower" Play a recording of *Swan Lake*. Tell children the story as they lie quietly. Repeat recording and have children dance "ballet." "One Misty, Moisty Morning"	"Robin in the Rain" and "5 Little Frogs," Raffi, *Singable Songs for the Very Young* *The Selfish Giant*, by Oscar Wilde "The Birds Know It Is Spring," *The Changing Seasons*, SVE

WEDNESDAY

Give each child a sack with a fruit, vegetable, or flower inside. Children take turns describing their item to the others. When the item is guessed, it can be removed from the sack.

Tape a piece of paper over a spring picture (a flower, a bird, etc.). See how quickly children guess what the picture is as you cut away the covering paper a small piece at a time.

Children make butterflies: Dip 2 coffee filters in different colors of water-color paints. Carefully push onto clothespin. Dry. Put on antennae made of a pipe cleaner.

 "Mistress Mary, Quite Contrary"

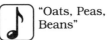

 "Oats, Peas, Beans"

 All About Seeds, by Susan Kuchalla

 "Snails, Whales, Ants and Plants," *Science, Unit 1*, Scholastic

 The Sunshine Book, by Helen Federico

THURSDAY

Take a walk outdoors (if spring has sprung) or look at appropriate filmstrip. Ask children to name changes they observe now that spring is here.

Children color a face on a plastic egg half. Fill with dirt and set inside a 2" x 6" circular band to avoid spilling. Plant grass seed and watch the egghead's hair grow!

Put a large paper on the wall. Children paint flowers to make a classroom garden scene. Encourage them to add birds, a sun, insects, and other spring things to the picture.

 "Robin Redbreast"

 "The Ants Go Marching"

 "White Coral Bells"

 "The Seed Story," *Tempo for Tots*

 The First Day of Spring, by Sharon Gordon

Bobby Bear in Spring, by Marilyn Helmrath and Janet Bartlett

FRIDAY

What do plants need to grow and be healthy? Where does rain come from? Sprout bean seeds in wet paper towel in a jar. Discuss the daily changes you see.

Make sound of rain by clapping, patting knees, pounding floor. Make rain with boiling water and a cold ladle from which condensed water drips.

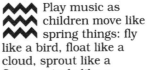 Put a dab of black *fingerpaint* on one corner of each child's paper and a dab of white on other corner. Have children fingerpaint rain clouds.

"Eensy, Weensy, Spider"

Play music as children move like spring things: fly like a bird, float like a cloud, sprout like a flower, wiggle like a worm.

 The Rain Puddle, by Adelaide Holl

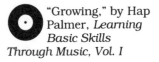 "Growing," by Hap Palmer, *Learning Basic Skills Through Music, Vol. I*

"Let's Guess: What Plant Is It?" *What Is It?* Encyclopedia Britannica

APRIL: WEEK 2
Babies are Born

	Thinking and Talking	Learning by Doing	Crafts and Creations	Songs and Games	Recommended Resources
MONDAY	Where do babies come from? Where are they born? Where do they grow? How do they come out? Mention ways different animal babies are born. Discuss names for baby animals: cat—kitten, dog—puppy, cow—calf, bear—cub, duck—duckling, goat—kid, and so on.	Bring baby clothes to school. Mix up in pile with children's clothes. Have each child pick an item, compare size, and decide if it belongs to baby or to child.	Trace outline of baby on construction paper *("Baby's Diaper")*. Have children cut out and paste on cloth triangle for diaper. Then they fill in facial features and create a toy out of paper for baby to hold, such as ball, rattle.	"Baby Grows" "Rock-a-bye Baby" 	*Once: A Lullaby*, by B. P. Nichols "Imagination," Rosenshontz, *Tickles You!* *Pig Grows Up*, by Donald McPhail
TUESDAY	Have children bring in picture of themselves as babies. Have class guess who each baby is. Children may ask questions. Is it a boy? Does he still have red hair?	Have children pair up. One pretends to be baby, other to be parent. Parent helps baby do buttons, zippers, laces, and so on. 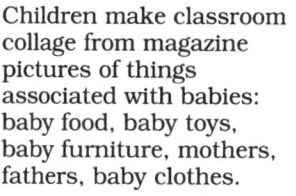	Children make classroom collage from magazine pictures of things associated with babies: baby food, baby toys, baby furniture, mothers, fathers, baby clothes.	"Bye Baby Bunting" Children have a crawling race through an obstacle course: around a chair, under a table, through a box, over a pillow.	*The New Baby*, by Ruth and Harold Shane *A New Baby Comes*, by Julian May "Sleep, Sleep," Rosenshontz, *Share It!*

WEDNESDAY

What can babies do? What can you do now that you couldn't do when you were a baby? Help children make a list of things they can do now.

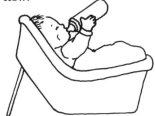

Give each child a hard-boiled egg on which they paint a face and paste a paper diaper. Tell children that they must take care of their egg baby all day long. Give stickers at end of day to "good parents."

Babies can't draw; they scribble. Have children make colorful scribbles on piece of paper pressing hard, and then paint over with weak black-tempera solution.

 "Here Is Baby's Tossled Head"

 "Hush, Little Baby"

 "Five Little Chickens"

 Before You Were a Baby, by Paul Showers

 "Something Old, Something New," *Science, Unit 1,* Scholastic

 Visit a hospital, or have a doctor visit the classroom. Invite a pregnant mother to class.

THURSDAY

What things do you need to care for a baby? Bring a bottle, blanket, diaper, lotion, stroller, and so on. Discuss why we need these items for a baby.

 Using feltboard, put baby animals in row *("Baby Animals").* Ask children which animal is first, second. Emphasize left-to-right direction. Match one number for each animal, counting how many, with felt numbers.

 Make *Baby's Applesauce.*

 "Five Little Mice"

 Play a record of lullabies. Tell children to listen. Are you sleepy? Children pretend to rock a baby to sleep.

 Nobody Asked Me If I Wanted a Baby Sister, by Martha Alexander

How You Were Born, by Joanna Cole

Have baby animals visit the classroom.

FRIDAY

Invite a parent to bring a real baby into class. Have baby be bathed or fed in front of class. Children ask parent questions about baby care. Discuss who can take care of babies. What can brothers and sisters do for baby?

 Give children a worksheet and have them draw a rattle for each baby to show 1-to-1 correspondence *("Rattles for Babies").*

Staple papers together in book form. Have children draw pictures of themselves and what they did as babies. Write down their dictated comments under each picture.

 "Sleep, Baby, Sleep"

 Children sit in circle with legs spread. They roll a ball back and forth as teacher directs: to a boy, to another boy, to a girl.

 Good Morning, Chick, by Mirra Ginsburg

 Who's in the Egg? by Alice and Martin Provensen

 "Mother Rabbit and Her Family," *Learning About Animals,* Encyclopedia Britannica

APRIL: WEEK 3
Old MacDonald

	Thinking and Talking	Learning by Doing	Crafts and Creations	Songs and Games	Recommended Resources
MONDAY	Show pictures of baby animals. Talk about food and care each animal must have. Discuss how different baby animals are born. Where do the farm babies live? What do animal babies eat? 	Sort plastic farm animals into same-kind groups. Count each group. "Do we have more cows or horses?" "More pigs or ducks?" 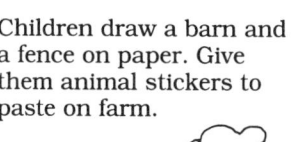	Turn cardboard box into barn. Cut door. Have children paint sides red and roof black. Make silo by wrapping paper around plastic bleach-bottle; put on cone-shaped top. Keep plastic farm animals inside.	"Baa, Baa, Black Sheep"  "Old MacDonald" 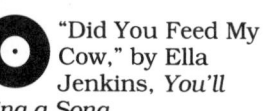 "This Little Calf"	*Too Much Noise,* by Ann McGovern 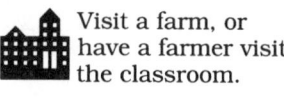 "Did You Feed My Cow," by Ella Jenkins, *You'll Sing a Song* 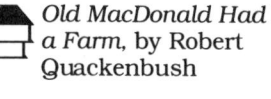 Visit a farm, or have a farmer visit the classroom. 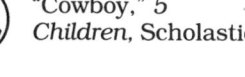
TUESDAY	How do different farm animals help us? A cow gives us milk, a sheep gives us wool, a chicken gives us eggs, and so on. 	Put out group of different farm animals. Children hide eyes while teacher removes one animal. Then children look and decide which animal is missing. 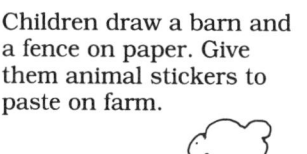	Children draw a barn and a fence on paper. Give them animal stickers to paste on farm. 	"Little Boy Blue" 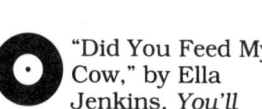 "Old Woman and the Pig" 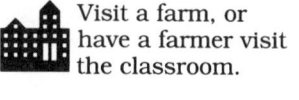 "Higgety-Piggety, My Black Hen" 	*Old MacDonald Had a Farm,* by Robert Quackenbush 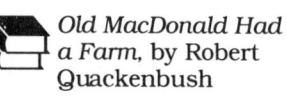 "Cowboy," *5 Children,* Scholastic 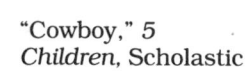 *Little Peep,* by Jack Kent 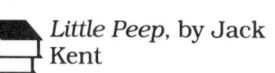 Bring a farm animal to school, or raise guinea pigs. 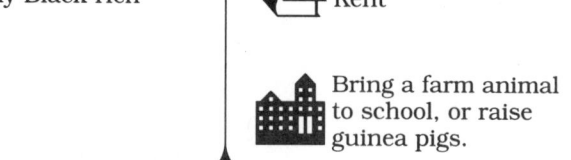

Clothespin a picture of animal onto back of each child's shirt. Child must guess animal by asking questions of other children. Am I big? Do I give milk?

 Give children worksheet with 1 hen and 1 chick in opposite corners ("Corn for the Chickens"). Have children paste corn kernels in straight line going from left to right connecting the two.

 Children paste small pieces of brown and white or black and white crushed tissue paper onto cow ("Cow Pattern").

 "This Little Pig"

 "The Farmer in the Dell"

 "Farmer"

 Rosie's Walk, by Pat Hutchins

Chester's Barn, by Lindee Clima

 "Pony Ride," *Preschool Fitness*

Show pictures of farm animals. Ask children to tell if each animal is bigger or smaller than they are.

Discuss what a farm, ranch, silo, hayloft, and so on are.

Paste pictures of various animals on cardboard. Put a paper clip on each. Children fish with magnet on string for picture. They name animal caught, imitate the sound it makes, and tell if it belongs on farm, in zoo, or at home.

 Children cut out traced pig and add curly tail made from tie tab ("Pig Pattern"). Then they paste pig on "mud" background made with thick brown poster paint (or brown shoe polish) on construction paper.

 "Can You Show Me How the Farmer?"

 "Animal Charades." Each child in turn imitates a farm animal (a trotting horse, a waddling duck, a walking cow) and the rest try to guess animal.

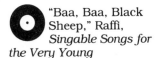 "Baa, Baa, Black Sheep," Raffi, *Singable Songs for the Very Young*

Three Billy Goats Gruff, Weston Woods

Ox-Cart Man, by Donald Hall

"Old MacDonald," *Disney's Children's Favorites, Vol. 1*

Am I telling the truth? Show pictures of objects and make absurd and true statements about them. Show cow and say, "I would find this in an apartment in the city." Or "This animal gives us wool."

 Make *Eggnog* and *French Toast*. Discuss milk and eggs from farm, bread from wheat, butter from cream.

Make *Clay*. Children model animals and let harden. Then they paint animals with poster paints.

 "Five Little Farmers"

 Children practice walking on balance beam over a blue paper "pond." Tell them to walk forward, backward, sideways. Don't fall into the pond!

The Very Busy Spider, by Eric Carle

Farm Alphabet Book, by Jane Miller

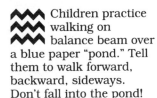 "On Rainbow Farm," *People Who Work, Unit 2*, Scholastic

APRIL: WEEK 4
Nature Calls

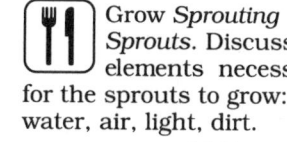

	Thinking and Talking	Learning by Doing	Crafts and Creations	Songs and Games	Recommended Resources
MONDAY	Take a "listening" walk. Walk, stop, and listen for one minute. Ask children to describe everything they heard. Listen again, harder. What new sounds do the children hear? 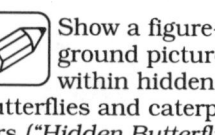	 Grow *Sprouting Sprouts*. Discuss elements necessary for the sprouts to grow: water, air, light, dirt. 	Help children make a class terrarium with collected rocks, earth, sand, mosses, and ferns. 	"Caterpillar"  "Six Little Ducks" "Whisky, Frisky" 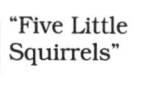	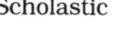 *Let's Grow a Garden*, by Gyo Fujikawa  "Bones Wings Teeth and Things," *Science*, Unit 1, Scholastic *All Butterflies*, by Marcia Brown
TUESDAY	Take a "looking" walk. Have children collect nature items to bring to class. Discuss caterpillar-to-butterfly and tadpole-to-frog cycles. Show pictures. Review plant growth and terms: leaf, stem, root, flower, seed, fruit.	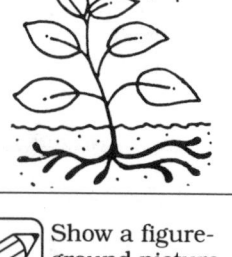 Show a figure-ground picture within hidden butterflies and caterpillars (*"Hidden Butterflies and Caterpillars"*). Have children find and color them.	Go for walk and have each child choose a favorite rock. Children paint rocks with designs, and teacher spray paints each with clear shellac. Children place them in a row from smallest to largest.	"Five Little Squirrels" Children panto-mime to music swaying trees, jumping frogs, crawling caterpillars, flying birds, blooming flowers.	"Garbage," Rosenshontz, *Share It!* *Cap'n Smudge* and *Bangalle* and *Serendipity*, by Stephen Cosgrove "Birds in the Circles," Hap Palmer, *Easy Does It*

Put earth in jar with sand on top. Put earthworms on top. Watch how they find their way down and leave castings.

Share an ant farm.

Put some nature objects collected in "looking" walk in grab bag. Have children take turns reaching in and holding something. Have them describe object out loud—hard, rough, heavy—and then try to name object.

Children make egg-carton caterpillars, using a pipe cleaner for antennae. Then they cover peanut with white yarn and attach to twig for cocoon.

 "My Garden"

 "Baby Bumblebee"

 "Over in the Meadow"

 "Hide and Seek" and "Sharing and Caring," *Science, Unit 1*, Scholastic

 The Plant Sitter, by Gene Zion

 Visit a forest or nature park.

Discuss different kinds of pollution: air, noise, water, land. Talk about how we can help eliminate or lessen pollution. Discuss the meaning of *biodegradable*. What types of things are biodegradable?

Go on walk with trash sacks. Collect paper. Clean up the playground and schoolyard.

Discuss noise pollution. Children make a collage of pictures of the culprits: motorcycles, big machines, loud radios, and so on.

 "Little Nut Tree"

 Children act out the cycle of a butterfly. Make a "cocoon" of stretchy material stitched together. Have children crawl inside, wiggle out, move about, and fly away.

 "Five Funny Speckled Frogs"

 How a Seed Grows, by Helene J. Jordan

 I Am a Mouse, by Ole Risom

 Have an artisan visit and demonstrate craft.

 "Funny Fat Frog," *Tempo for Tots*

Classify and graph items collected on "looking" walk by color, kind, size, whether they sink or float, and whether they are rough or smooth.

 Make a *Garden Salad* using your sprouts.

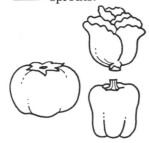

 Give children out-of-sequence pictures of developing stages of a butterfly, plant, or frog (*"From Tadpole to Frog"*). Have the children color them, cut them out, paste them in the proper sequence.

 Play record of jazz and record of folk music. Ask children which they prefer.

 "My Turtle"

Have a birdcaller visit the class.

Over in the Meadow, by John Langstaff and Feodor Rojankovsky

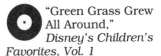 "Green Grass Grew All Around," *Disney's Children's Favorites, Vol. 1*

MAY: WEEK 1
Trains and Boats and Planes

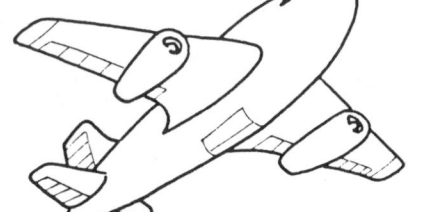

	Thinking and Talking	Learning by Doing	Crafts and Creations	Songs and Games	Recommended Resources
MONDAY	What does the word *transportation* mean? What kinds of transportation can you think of? What is a vehicle? Name all vehicles you can. Have children sort several objects into 2 piles—or put in 2 baskets—of vehicles and nonvehicles. Discuss and sort pictures of vehicles that float and those that don't.	Children make binoculars by putting a rubber band around 2 cardboard toilet-paper rolls and painting. Look through your new binoculars and tell what you see.	Give children 2–3 spoonfuls of paint on large paper. They enjoy "racing" tiny cars through the paint, making designs on the paper. Cars are easily cleaned with soapy water.	"Ride a Cock Horse" "Down by the Station" 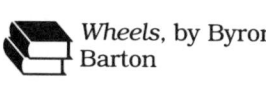	 *The Little Engine That Could,* by Watty Piper  *"Curious George Rides a Bike,"* Weston Woods "Rowing" and "Helicopter Twirl," *Preschool Fitness*
TUESDAY	Set up an electric train set. Discuss the various cars and their purpose. Each child brings a toy vehicle from home. Sort them by size, color, and type. Line them up from largest to smallest. Whose is first, second, third, last? 	Make cardboard or plywood hills for small toy vehicles. Whose can get down first? Which hill is steeper? Switch cars; now whose gets to the bottom first? Why?	Children make *Apple Sailboats* from an apple slice, a triangular piece of cheese, and a toothpick. Eat for snack. 	"Choo-choo Train" Children use whistles and bells to give transportation signals: long and short, loud and soft, near and far.	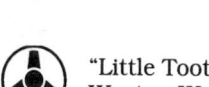 *Wheels,* by Byron Barton "Little Toot" Weston Woods Ride a train, boat, or bus.

How do objects look from an airplane, a fast car, or a train? (smaller or blurred) Show pictures of vehicles. Which means of transportation do you know? Have you traveled in a boat, car, airplane, taxi, submarine, rocket ship, canoe, camper? Which is fastest, slowest, most fun?

 Give children a worksheet with pictures of vehicles with wheels missing *("Wheels")*. Children draw in correct number of wheels in their proper place.

Children make and fly paper airplanes. Which ones fly faster, higher, dive down more? Bend tail wings slightly. What happens?

 "Airplane"

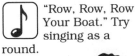

 "Row, Row, Row Your Boat." Try singing as a round.

 Freight Train, by Donald Crews

Have a conductor or driver visit the class.

Train Whistles, by Helen Sattler

What safety rules are important when traveling? Why? Mention seat belts, traffic signs.

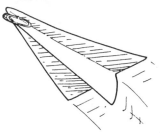 Put picture of a student behind the cut-out window of an engine pattern *("Train and Engineer")*. Cover the window with "curtain" and slowly expose face from top to bottom. Who's driving the train?

Make cars and taxis that children can wear over shoulders. Cut away top and bottom of cardboard box. Make shoulder straps with rope. Cut out cardboard wheels from these pieces and paste on vehicle. Have children paint, adding desired details. Have them line up their cars. Who is first, second, third, last?

 "I've Been Working on the Railroad"

 Children go through an obstacle course imitating a car, horse, train, airplane.

 "Merrily We Roll Along"

 Little Toot, by Hardie Gramatky

 "Row, Row, Row" and "Bicycle Built for Two," *Disney's Children's Favorites, Vol. 1*

Beat Book, by Gail Gibbons

Show pictures of old-fashioned modes of transportation. Compare to transportation today. Ask what children think vehicles will look like a long time from now. Discuss creating pollution-free vehicles.

Give children various wood scraps, spools, pop lids, string, pipe cleaners, and glue. Supervise as children hammer and glue pieces to make the "car of the future." Children paint finished cars. Line them up for a new car parade.

Children invent new types of vehicles by tracing shape templates. Have children tell you where vehicles will travel: air, land, water, underground.

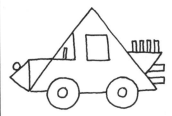

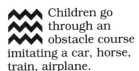 "My Bicycle"

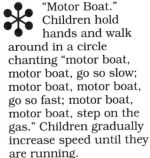 "Motor Boat." Children hold hands and walk around in a circle chanting "motor boat, motor boat, go so slow; motor boat, motor boat, go so fast; motor boat, motor boat, step on the gas." Children gradually increase speed until they are running.

 Trucks You Can Count On, by Doug Magee

Boats, by Anne Rockwell

 "How Are We Going?" Hap Palmer, *Learning Basic Skills Through Music: Vocabulary*

"Jet Pilot," *People Who Work, Unit 2,* Scholastic

MAY: WEEK 2
Blast-off

	Thinking and Talking	Learning by Doing	Crafts and Creations	Songs and Games	Recommended Resources
MONDAY	Bring a big globe to class. Ask children to tell you what they think the blue parts and the other parts are. Explore globe together. Show children where they are now; point out other places.	Make worksheet of colored stars and circles (planets; *"Space Shapes"*). Ask children to draw the shape that comes next. Emphasize left-to-right progression.	Begin making a papier-mâché globe on top of large balloon. Children work together to put pieces of papier mâché over balloon. When globe is dry, children paint land masses and water that teacher draws.	"Starlight, Star Bright" "Moon Walk." Tape footprints on the floor to show children where to step on their moon walk. Make footprints far enough apart so they will have to leap from one to another.	*Our Friend the Sun,* by Janet Palazzo *Goodnight Moon,* by Margaret Wise Brown *Wynken, Blynken and Nod,"* Weston Woods
TUESDAY	How does the sun help us? Answers can include telling time, food for plants, warmth, dry clothes.	Use photoprint paper to make art prints. Put child-selected objects on paper. Put in sun. Look at results of sun's light.	Children design and make spaceships from plastic bottles and other containers, plus cardboard, aluminum foil, and paints.	"Sally Go Round the Sun" "Moonrocks Hunt." Make "moonrocks" from balls of aluminum foil. Hide on playground or in classroom. How many moonrocks can you find? Where were they? "The Evening Is Coming"	*Many Moons,* by James Thurber Visit a science museum, planetarium, or airport. *Trouble in Space,* by Rose Greydanus and Don Page

WEDNESDAY

What else is present in space besides our earth and sun? (Answers include moon, planets.) Show pictures of planets and a star map. Ask children for comments. Are these things close to us or far away? When do we see the moon? the sun? (day and night)

Make space-creature puppets from paper bags. Children close eyes, and one child is chosen to go behind stage. With only puppet showing, child pretends to be from another planet and "moon talks" (like someone from outer space). Others guess who it is.

Make "cloud pictures" by pasting cotton on sky background colored or painted by children. Remind children that there are times when sky is not blue: sunrise, sunset, storm. Encourage them to paint sky other colors.

 "If All the World Were Paper"

 Children try to keep white balloons "floating in the sky." How long can you keep your balloon in the air?

 Have a pilot visit the classroom.

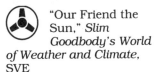 "Aiken Drum," and "Mr. Sun," Raffi, *Singable Songs for the Very Young.*

 "Our Friend the Sun," *Slim Goodbody's World of Weather and Climate*, SVE

THURSDAY

How do we get up in space? Show pictures of different spaceships. How do astronauts communicate with earth? How do spaceships fly differently from normal airplanes.

Talk about gravity. Children make parachutes with paper napkins and string attached to each corner with adhesive tape to aluminum foil space capsule. Drop from stairs or ladder.

Children make a constellation by cutting, pasting, and decorating various sizes of circles with glitter. Hang on a clothesline.

 "Twinkle, Twinkle, Little Star"

Children pretend they are spaceships. They crouch down and count backward from 10. At zero, or "blast-off," they jump as high as they can. Children lie quietly on the floor, pretending to be floating in space as they listen to soft music.

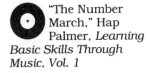 *Why the Sun and the Moon Live in the Sky*, by Elphinstone Dayrell

 "The Number March," Hap Palmer, *Learning Basic Skills Through Music, Vol. 1*

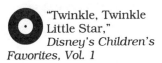 *Happy Birthday, Moon* and *Mooncake*, by Frank Asch

FRIDAY

How is space different from our earth's atmosphere? Would you like to go into space? Why? Why not? Make a picture graph of children who would and would not like to go. Count them.

 Cook and eat dehydrated foods like astronauts. Idea: *"Astronaut Roll-ups."*

Children make spaceships with toothpicks, marsh-mallows, and chickpeas that have been soaked overnight. They then decorate round plastic margarine lids for flying saucers.

 Children jump on a trampoline or a big mattress and pretend they are jumping in space.

 "5 Little Monkeys Jumping on the Bed"

 "Blastoff"

 "Twinkle, Twinkle Little Star," *Disney's Children's Favorites, Vol. 1*

Meteor, by Patricia Polacco

"The Changing Earth and Sky" and "Down to Earth," *Science, Unit 2*, Scholastic

MAY: WEEK 3
Goin' to the Zoo

	Thinking and Talking	Learning by Doing	Crafts and Creations	Songs and Games	Recommended Resources
MONDAY	Show children pictures and ask, What animals do we find in the zoo? Where do these animals come from? Which ones are dangerous? Which ones are fast? Which slow? What sounds do they make? Which ones are loud?	Children use bright tempera colors to paint a jungle mural. Some can paint trees, some the sky, some flowers. Each child paints his or her favorite jungle animal. Locate items at the top, in the middle, and at the bottom of the mural and identify.	Children make "paper-plate elephants." They draw eyes on paper plate and glue on ears that they have traced and cut out. Then they fold a strip of paper back and forth accordion-style and glue it on for the nose. Use as a mask puppet.	"The Zoo" "5 Little Monkeys Swinging in a Tree" Draw an elephant face on a large plastic bottle. Children drop peanuts into the container. How many peanuts did you feed the elephant?	*Have You Seen My Duckling*, by Nancy Tafuri "Baby Zoo Animals," *Baby Animals in Rhyme and Song*, SVE *Come to the Zoo*, by Ruth Jensen "Animal Fair," *Disney's Children's Favorites, Vol. 1*
TUESDAY	Different animals need different shelters for reasons of climate, habits, size. Discuss, using pictures.	Hide pictures of animals on playground. Children go on a safari and "catch" animals. They try to guess classmates' animals by asking questions such as, Is it a big animal? Does it live in jungle? Does it have a trunk?	 Children model animals out of *clay*. When animals are hard, they paint them and put them in shoebox cages.	"I Am an Elephant" Children pretend they are flamingos and balance on one foot. How long can you balance?	"Animal Alphabet," Alan Mills, *14 Numbers, Letters and Animal Songs* *If I Ran the Zoo*, by Dr. Seuss "Remembering a Zoo," *Developing Visual Memory*, SVE

Play a rhyming game. Make up poems about zoo animals and omit last word, which is animal's name. Children supply this word. "He can roar loud, without even tryin'. His name is the mighty ___" (lion).

Give children a worksheet and have them match animal groups to the correct numeral *("Counting Animals")*.

Children make zoo pins by varnishing an animal cracker and gluing it to a fastener on the back. Wear your favorite zoo animal!

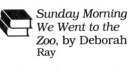 "If I Were a Horse"

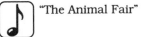 "The Animal Fair"

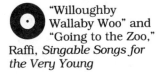 *Sunday Morning We Went to the Zoo*, by Deborah Ray

 "Willoughby Wallaby Woo" and "Going to the Zoo," Raffi, *Singable Songs for the Very Young*

Zoo Animals, by Michele Chopin Roosevelt

Using pictures, compare animals in size, color, and other characteristics. Use comparative and superlative adjectives. "The lion is the fiercest animal." "The elephant is bigger than the buffalo."

Give children pictures of animal homes and habitats *("Animal Homes")*. They match animals to their homes.

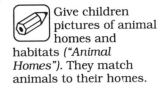

 Children make *Monkey Sandwiches*. They make peanut butter and spread it on bananas.

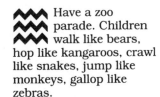

 "Way Down South"

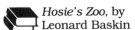 "I Wish I Was" and "Hippopotamus Rock," Rosenshontz, *Tickles You!*

Hosie's Zoo, by Leonard Baskin

Animal Games, by Brian Wildsmith

Put pile of plastic animals or pictures of animals in center of circle. Have children separate them into groups: farm animals, pets, zoo animals. Discuss characteristics they have in common. Group also by color and size.

Play tape of animal sounds. Have children guess what animal it is. Or have children take turns imitating an animal while other children try to guess what it is.

Children invent new animals. Fold paper in 3 parts. One child draws animal's head. Next child draws body, without seeing head. Last child draws legs and feet without seeing head and body.

 "The Kangaroo"

 Have a zoo parade. Children walk like bears, hop like kangaroos, crawl like snakes, jump like monkeys, gallop like zebras.

 "Tiger Walk"

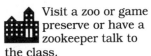 "Jumbo Elephant," *Preschool Fitness*

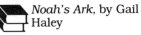 Visit a zoo or game preserve or have a zookeeper talk to the class.

Noah's Ark, by Gail Haley

MAY: WEEK 4
Vacation Time

SKILLS TO INTRODUCE

- Identify seasonal changes (S)
- Describe weather, using terms such as sunny, rainy, cold (S)
- Give examples and reasons for school and community rules (SS)
- Name and associate objects of clothing (SS)
- Comprehend and follow basic safety rules (SS)
- Recite address and telephone number (LA)
- Follow directions (LA)
- Recognize objects as same and different (LA)
- Extend a demonstrated pattern (M)
- Explore and create with rhythm instruments (Mu)
- Create pictures with paints (A)
- Demonstrate ability to change directions and go around obstacles while running (PE)

	Thinking and Talking	**Learning by Doing**	**Crafts and Creations**	**Songs and Games**	**Recommended Resources**
MONDAY	What is the weather like in the summer? What can we do in summer that we cannot do in other seasons? Make a word and picture list. 	On feltboard match pieces of clothing to appropriate weather (*"Winter Clothes and Summer Clothes"*). 	Children make sand pictures by drawing design on paper with glue, sprinkling sand on picture, and shaking off excess. 	"Five Little Seashells" "T-Ball." In this simplified form of baseball, children hit plastic ball set on "T" frame and run around the 3 bases. They can chant "Take Me Out to the Ballgame" as they play.	*Play Ball, Kate,* by Sharon Gordon *Blue Bug's Surprise,* by Virginia Poulet "Fisherman's Son," *Five Children,* Scholastic "Take Me Out to the Ballgame," *Disney's Children's Favorites*
TUESDAY	What special rules must we follow in summer? for swimming? for being in the sun? when traveling? 	Children make *Ants on a Log.* Go outside and have a picnic (snack) on blankets. 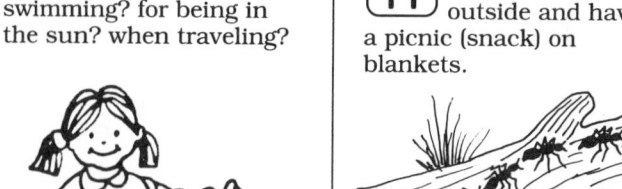	If day is sunny, children go outside and blow bubbles (*"Bubble Solution"*). Look at colors in bubbles. If indoors, put paint in bubble solution. Children make bubbles and let them burst on construction paper to make bubble paintings. 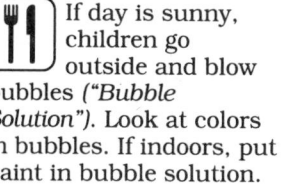	"Golden Fishes" 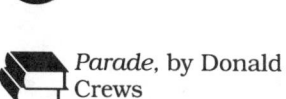 Play catch outside with water balloons.	*The SeaView Hotel,* by James Stevenson "Catch a Firefly," *Preschool Fitness* *Parade,* by Donald Crews

WEDNESDAY	What is a vacation? Ask children what they plan to do for their summer vacation. 	Play "I packed my grandmother's trunk, and in it I put . . ." Each child renames previous items and adds a new item. How many items can the children remember? 	Children use whole and broken seashells to make collages.	"The Very Nicest Place" Play "Follow the Leader" with rhythm instruments. Leader indicates when to play loud or soft.	*Summer Story*, by Jill Barklem *Whistle for Willie*, Weston Woods Take a picnic. Go to a recreation center or park. 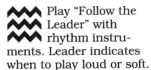 *Summer*, by Colin McNaughton

THURSDAY	Have children dictate telephone number and address for teacher to copy on small cards to give to their friends. Make a list to send home so children leaving for the summer can invite friends over to play.	Have children sort various types of balls (tennis balls, Ping-Pong balls, baseballs, basketballs, beach balls, and so on) and group into like sets. Repeat with sports caps and helmets.	Children draw face on popsicle sticks and make *Popsicles*. Check every 10 minutes to see how long it takes for them to freeze.	"Swinging" Organize a "mini-Olympics." Have relay races and obstacle-course races. Give ribbons to *all* participants. "The Snail"	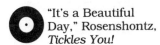 *Emilio's Summer Day*, by Miriam Ann Bourne "Gonna Have a Good Time" and "Going Away," Rosenshontz, *Share It!* "In the Good Old Summertime," *Disney's Children's Favorites, Vol. 1*

FRIDAY	Give children 3- or 4-step directions; for example, untie your shoe, walk to the door, sit down, and say "Boo!" (Keep directions fun!)	Put 3 colors of fish with paper clips in pond on floor. Catch fish in order: orange, blue, yellow. Children take turns fishing for the correct color with a pole with magnet on the end. Hang fish in proper color sequence. 	Children *finger-paint* a blue ocean. When it is dry, they draw fish with chalk. 	"This Is What I Can Do" 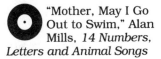 "Little Sally Saucer"	"It's a Beautiful Day," Rosenshontz, *Tickles You!* "Mother, May I Go Out to Swim," Alan Mills, *14 Numbers, Letters and Animal Songs* "Summer," *Seasonal Adventures of the Lollipop Dragon,* SVE

JUNE: WEEK 1
Fatal Attraction

	Thinking and Talking	Learning by Doing	Crafts and Creations	Songs and Games	Recommended Resources
MONDAY	Using a fishing pole made with a dowel, string, and magnet, pick up colorful paper fish that have paper clips attached. Ask the children how they think this is possible. Take paper clips off the fish and see what happens.	Place various pictures of body parts on the floor with a paper clip fastened on each. Children use the fishing pole to pick up pictures of body parts. After each "catch," the child names the body part and one of its uses.	Children draw and cut out their favorite story scenes and characters. Put a small magnetic strip on the back of each character. Children can use a metal chalkboard or file cabinet to hang their pictures in proper sequence and tell their favorite story.	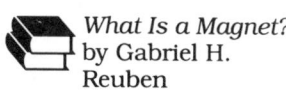 "Five Little Magnets" 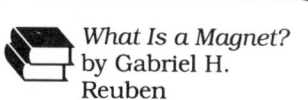 "Who Has the Magnet." One child leaves room while rest of children pass a magnet around the circle to music. When music stops, "it" returns and tries to guess who has magnet. 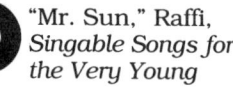 "Touch My Hair"	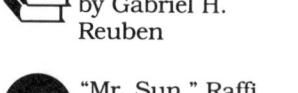 *What Is a Magnet?* by Gabriel H. Reuben 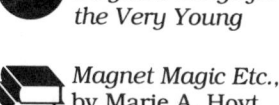 "Mr. Sun," Raffi, *Singable Songs for the Very Young*  *Magnet Magic Etc.,* by Marie A. Hoyt
TUESDAY	Bring as many types of magnets to class as possible: bar magnets, horseshoe magnets, ring magnets, disc magnets. Talk about their different shapes and sizes. Demonstrate a compass, and point out north, south, east, and west. Explain that a compass points north because mineral deposits (metals) are more abundant there.	Put many different magnets out for the children to explore with freely. Observe as children discover for themselves that certain "sides" of magnets attract and others repel.  [S N] [S N] 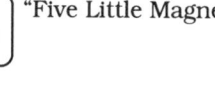	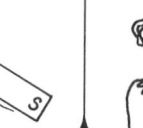 Children make horseshoe-magnet biscuits. Give each child some *Bendable Biscuit* dough to roll and shape into a horseshoe. Bake and eat for snack. 	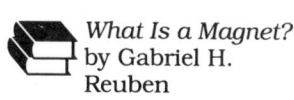 "Swing Them" 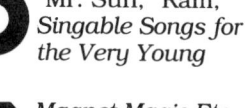 Put names of favorite class songs and picture clue on cards with paper clips. Children take turns "fishing" for a song with the magnetic fishing pole. Sing each song that is caught.	 "Discovering Magnets," *Discovering Magnets and Electricity,* SVE 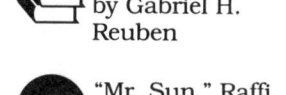 *Mickey's Magnet,* by Franklyn Branley and Eleanor Vaughn 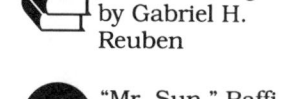 *The Real Magnet Book,* by Mae Freeman

WEDNESDAY

Use magnets to demonstrate and discuss these concepts:
- magnets have two poles;
- the magnet's attraction is strongest at its poles;
- similar poles repel and opposite poles attract.

Children can experiment with these concepts.

Put two trays on a table and label them "yes" and "no." Children experiment with magnets and different objects, sorting objects into the appropriate tray. Ask children if they can determine any common characteristics among the items that were picked up by the magnet.

Children make collages using only objects that will be picked up by magnets, such as paper clips, pieces of wire, small nails, washers, and metal lids. Check items for sharp points.

 One child is a "magnet" and all others are "metal objects." Magnet runs about room, changing directions often and others follow him or her.

 "My Hands"

 Light, by Don Crews

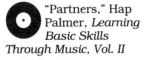 "Partners," Hap Palmer, *Learning Basic Skills Through Music, Vol. II*

Observe a scientist performing experiments with magnets.

THURSDAY

Ask children to name objects in the room that will be attracted by a magnet. Hold up different objects and ask if a magnet will pick it up. Have children take turns testing.

Give each child a piece of thin cardboard on which to draw a road. Have them put a metal ring, paper clip, or other metal object on the road and try to "drive" it from one end to the other, using a magnet held on the bottom side of the cardboard.

Instead of iron filings, make crayon filings. Help children grate old crayons with a cheese grater. Children arrange on a paper. Bake at low heat to melt crayon filings, and let cool.

 Divide children into two teams and give each team a magnet. Children line up and have a relay race. The first child on each team climbs a jungle gym and sticks a magnet on the top bar. The second child on each team climbs to the top to retrieve the magnet, and so on.

 "There Was a Crooked Man"

 Visit a science museum.

Swimmy, by Leo Lionni

North, South, East, and West, by Franklyn M. Branley

FRIDAY

Discuss how magnets can be useful: refrigerator note-holders, can openers, magnetic letters and numbers, and so on. Bring examples to share with the children. Ask children to name ways in which a compass is useful.

Give children magnetic numerals and objects to group into sets on a metal chalkboard or file cabinet. Can they count the number of objects in each set and match the number that corresponds to each set?

Children make refrigerator magnets by decorating clip clothespins with felt-tip markers and gluing a magnetic strip on the back side. Great for hanging artwork on the fridge!

 "Thumbkin Says, 'I'll Dance'"

 Label and point out north, south, east, and west on classroom walls. Lead children in movements in different directions: "march north," "hop south," "run east," "walk west."

 "Right Hand, Left Hand"

"Touch" and "Left and Right," Hap Palmer, *Getting to Know Myself*

The Magic Fish, by Freya Littledale

 "What's Going On?—Energy," *Science, Unit 2*, Scholastic

JUNE: WEEK 2
Once Upon A Time

SKILLS TO INTRODUCE

- Identify emotions and feelings (SS)
- Follow directions (LA)
- Tell a simple story (LA)
- Identify rhyming words (LA)
- Recite simple poems and rhymes (LA)
- Sequence events from a story (LA)
- Recall details from a story (LA)
- Compare sets to determine if they have more, less, or equal number of members (M)
- Sing class songs from memory (Mu)
- Work with classmates on group art projects (A)
- Roll body in coordinated way (PE)

	Thinking and Talking	Learning by Doing	Crafts and Creations	Songs and Games	Recommended Resources
MONDAY	Read a favorite fairy tale to the class. Ask if they believe this story really happened. What impossible things occurred in the story? Were there any make-believe characters in the story? 	Children cut out magazine pictures of real and pretend things. Make a collage of real things and a collage of pretend things. Count and determine if the children found more real or pretend items.	Children make crowns by cutting out construction paper strips and decorating with glue and glitter. Staple together to fit each child's head. 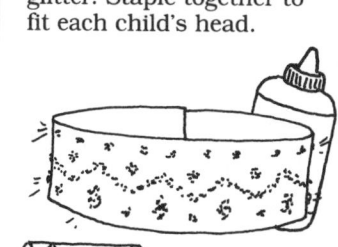	"Old King Cole." Children may enjoy wearing their crowns as they sing this one. "Diddle, Diddle, Dumpling" "Little Miss Muffet"	*Cinderella*, retold by Amy Erlich See a children's theater production. "Who's Afraid of the Big Bad Wolf?" Rosenshontz, *Share It!*
TUESDAY	Discuss what is the same about most fairy tales: (1) They begin with "once upon a time"; (2) they have a beginning and usually a happy ending; (3) they often have a "bad guy"; (4) many times there are queens, kings, fairies, and magical animals. Ask what kinds of feelings the children have when they listen to fairy tales.	Pass out pictures of rhyming words. Help children look for a friend who has a picture that rhymes with their picture. Rhyming friends sit down together in circle. 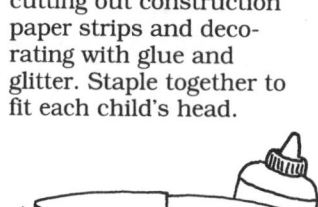	Working in small groups, children create castles from shoe boxes, paper rolls, match boxes, and other cardboard items. Children can decorate castles with tempera paint, or teacher can spray castles silver, and children can decorate with markers. Doors and windows can be drawn or made from construction paper.	"Oh Where Has My Little Dog Gone?" "Little Bo-Peep" 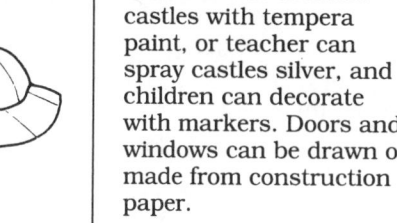	*Tomie de Paola's Favorite Nursery Tales*, by Tomie de Paola "Tickles You" and "Imagination," Rosenshontz, *Tickles You!* Have a puppeteer visit, or go to a puppet show.

WEDNESDAY

Recite familiar nursery rhymes together. Talk about rhyming words. Read lines and have children supply the missing rhyming word. Examples: There was a *cat* who chased a ___. "Tick, tock, tick, *tock*," says the big ___. I had a little bear and his name was Tiny *Tim*; I threw him in the pond to see if he could ___. Make up new rhyming lines.

Invite older children or special friends to visit the classroom to read their favorite fairy tale to the class. Who is the favorite character?

Children make puppets of nursery rhyme characters by drawing and coloring faces on paper plates. Glue or tape on a tongue depressor. Eyes can be cut out to make mask.

 Children take turns being king and queen, sitting on a "throne" (decorated chair) and giving their "subjects" royal commands such as "do a somersault, roll over and over like a log, hop on one foot three times."

 "Long, Long Ago"

 "Emperor's New Clothes," "Jack and the Beanstalk," and "The Musicians of Bremen," *Katharine Hepburn's Tales of Wit and Wisdom*, SVE

The Ugly Duckling, by Hans Christian Anderson, illustrated by Monika Laimgruber

Puss in Boots, by Paul Galdone

THURSDAY

Brainstorm ideas for an original class fairy tale. Ask children, Who should be the most important character? Who will be the bad guy? What will happen in our story? Will there be a hero or heroine? Each child tells a small part of the story, which the teacher writes on a large paper. Reread the story together.

Each child dictates a fairy tale for the teacher to write or type. Each child draws or paints an illustration for his or her story.

Children draw or paint pictures of the meanest or scariest fairy tale villain that they can imagine: A wolf, a witch, a bad king, a troll, and so on.

 "Wolf." One child, the "wolf," hides as others chant, "Wolf, are you ready?" Wolf replies, "Not yet; first I have to comb my hair," and pretends to comb hair. Children repeat chant as wolf ties shoes, puts on coat, and so on. Finally, wolf says, "I'm coming," and chases others and catches a new wolf.

 "Little Tom Tinker"

The Five Chinese Brothers, by Claire Huchet Bishop and Kurt Wiese

Snow White and the Seven Dwarfs, retold by Freya Littledale

 "The Friendly Giant," Hap Palmer, *Pretend*

FRIDAY

Read a favorite fairy tale. Ask the children to retell this story. What happened first, second, and in the end? Ask each child to name his or her favorite story. Children can dramatize the most popular fairy tale.

 Demonstrate how to make *Curds and Whey*. Children make spiders by gluing pipe cleaner pieces to bottom half of walnut shell and painting black. They take turns sitting on a tuffet (clump of grass) and dramatizing "Little Miss Muffett." Spread remainder of curds and whey on crackers for snack.

Make a puppet stage by cutting an opening in a large appliance box. Children paint with tempera paint. When stage is dry, each child uses felt-tip markers to decorate the stage with his or her favorite nursery rhyme or fairy tale character. Make a curtain with an old pillowcase or piece of fabric. Have a puppet show!

 "For He's (She's) a Jolly Good Fellow"

 "Ding, Dong Bell"

 Recite favorite nursery rhymes and have children imitate actions: sitting on a clinker, wagging tails, jumping candlesticks, tumbling down hill, sleeping under haystack. Emphasize sequences of events.

Three Billy Goats Gruff, retold by Paul Galdone

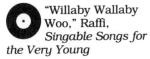 "Willaby Wallaby Woo," Raffi, *Singable Songs for the Very Young*

 "Beauty and the Beast," Weston Woods

JUNE: WEEK 3
One, Two, Buckle My Shoe

	Thinking and Talking	Learning by Doing	Crafts and Creations	Songs and Games	Recommended Sources
MONDAY	Show large cardboard numerals. Ask, What are these? What do we use numbers for? Where are some places that we find numbers? Bring several objects that have numbers to share with the children, such as clocks, signs, coins, rulers, books, license plates, telephones, watches, and calendars.	Count various objects in the classroom together. Make a picture chart illustrating the number of chairs, tables, trucks, dolls, and so on. Set out cardboard circles with numbers around the edge and clothespins with a number on each. Children clip clothespins to matching numbers on cardboard circles.	Children cut out numbers from magazines and newspapers, and paste them on a sheet of paper to make a number collage. 	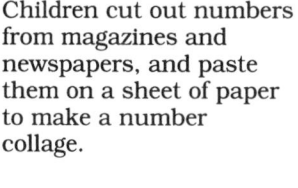 "Two Little Blackbirds" ♪ "This Old Man" ✌ "Five Little Puppies"	📚 *Count and See,* by Tana Hoban 🎞 "Learning about Counting and Colors," *The Merry-Mouse School Days,* SVE 💿 "Farmer Brown Had Ten Green Apples," Alan Mills, *14 Numbers, Letters and Animal Songs*
TUESDAY	Children take turns asking "how-many" questions: How many buttons are on your shirt? How many eyes do you have? How many girls are in the room? How many boys are in the room? How far can we count? Children sit in circle and count off, with each child reciting the next number. Count together in a Papa Bear voice, Mama Bear voice, Baby Bear voice.	Children take home a "counting questionnaire" to fill out with their parents. Each child should count how many beds, dogs, trucks, brothers, sisters, televisions, refrigerators, bathtubs are in the household. Parents can assist by writing the number beside the corresponding picture. In which room was each object found?	Give children a large piece of paper and set of multicolored paints and direct them to make an ugly monster with two huge heads, three eyes, four ears, six arms, one leg, and no mouth! Let them describe their finished monsters.	♪ "Phone Number Song" ✌ "Left to the Window" 〰 Children pick a number out of a hat and perform a movement the designated number of times. (Hop three times, clap two times, and so on.)	📚 *1 Hunter,* by Pat Hutchins 📚 *Ten, Nine, Eight,* by Molly Bang ✉ "Nimble Numbers," Kimbo

WEDNESDAY

Toss a handful of a few beans and a handful of many beans on floor. Children identify which pile has "few" and which has "many." Ask children to guess how many beans are in each pile. Count the beans together. How many beans are there altogether?

Give each child an empty egg carton with a number written inside each compartment, and a cup of beans. Children fill each section with the proper number of beans. Help children count beans to see if they counted correctly.

Children make books about their family, drawing one member of the family on each page. Write name of the family member below each picture. Who has the largest family? Who is the youngest person in each family? the oldest? How are the families different? How are the families alike?

 "Four Little Monkeys"

 "Beehive"

 Children take turns bouncing balls with two hands while classmates count. Bring several types of balls outside; have children identify which can be rolled, batted, served, putted, thrown, rolled, dribbled.

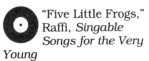 "Five Little Frogs," Raffi, *Singable Songs for the Very Young*

Anno's Counting House, by Anno Mitsumasa

Take a counting walk. Count how many trees or how many animals you pass.

THURSDAY

Show children a telephone with a phone number typed on it. Ask, What is this? What is it used for? Why is it important for us to learn our telephone numbers? Make a large telephone number card for each child to take home to practice reciting. Make a class phone number directory, writing numbers as children dictate.

Class makes individual *Cereal Snack Sacks* from a recipe with rebus clues. Children can count each kind of cereal as designated in the recipe and mix in a cup. Eat for snack.

Children state their addresses. Print each child's address at the top of a large piece of paper. Beneath address, children paint a watercolor picture of where they live.

1234 Center Street

 "Hands on Shoulders"

 Children practice self-help skills of buttoning, zipping, lacing by "racing" against a timer. Ask children to guess how long it will take them to put on coat, lace shoes, and so on.

 "One, Two, Buckle My Shoe"

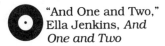 "Lucky Numbers," Hap Palmer, *Learning Basic Skills Through Music, Vol II*

Brian Wildsmith's 1, 2, 3's, by Brian Wildsmith

"And One and Two," Ella Jenkins, *And One and Two*

FRIDAY

Ask children, How many is a million? Could you eat a million cookies? What would you like to have a million of? Can someone be a million years old? How old are you?

Children take turns measuring each other using Unifix cubes. Compare length of Unifix "measures." Who is the tallest? the shortest? Can someone measure the teacher?

Children bend pipe cleaners to form numbers and glue them onto paper. Children enjoy drawing funny faces on the numbers, making number people.

 "I Caught A Fish Alive"

 Introduce jump rope to the children. Wiggle it like a snake on the floor for the children to jump over. Raise it a few inches from the ground for children to leap over. Mature children can try jumping with rope and singing counting rhymes.

Count on Calico Cat, by Donald Charles

How Much Is a Million? by David M. Schwartz

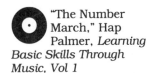 "The Number March," Hap Palmer, *Learning Basic Skills Through Music, Vol 1*

JUNE: WEEK 4
Bang, Clip, Whir

	Thinking and Talking	Learning by Doing	Crafts and Creations	Songs and Games	Recommended Resources
MONDAY	Present children with a tray full of assorted tools: garden, household, woodworking. Ask, What are these called? What are they for? Pick up each tool, one by one, and help children identify and state its purpose.	Give children trays filled with nuts and bolts of various sizes to sort and connect. 	Children use classroom tools—scissors, ruler, paper punch, and stapler—to cut, fold, and staple various types of paper and fabric to make a paper collage or a picture of something they would like to build.	♪ "Johnny Pounds with One Hammer" ❀ "There's Music in a Hammer"	*Tool Book*, by Gail Gibbons *Crash! Bang! Boom!* by Peter Spier "Cutting Wood," *Preschool Fitness*
TUESDAY	Discuss how tools make jobs easier. What tools would we use to bake a cake? Plant seeds? Build a boat? What workers in our community use tools? Which tools? 	Make *Pudding Tarts*, using a hand beater, a wire whisk, and an electric mixer. Which is faster? Why?	With adult supervision, children saw off a small block of wood, then glue a piece of heavy string on it in a design of their choice. Dip in tempera paint and print designs on construction paper.	Children use their bodies to imitate movement of different tools to different instrumental rhythms: slowly turn round and round like a screwdriver, bend at waist and bob up and down like a hammer, arms chop like scissors, and so on. ✌ "Dig a Little Hole"	*Fix-It*, by David McPhail 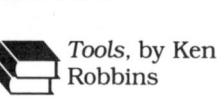 Take a supervised visit to a construction site, or have a carpenter visit the classroom. *Tools*, by Ken Robbins

WEDNESDAY

Give children a large variety of tools to sort into sets. (Avoid any with sharp points or edges.) Classify by size, color, and function.

Using gardener's tools, plant a small garden—dig holes, plant seeds, rake, water, and so on. Sequence and label actions: What are you doing now Jim? What will we do after we put this seed in the hole? What will we do next?

 Children free-explore with *clay* and a variety of clay tools.

 "Hokey Pokey"

 "Hammering"

Dig, Drill, Dump, Fill, by Tana Hoban

"Mike Mulligan and His Steam Shovel," Weston Woods

Visit a hardware store.

THURSDAY

Put tools (no sharp ones) into large bag. Children take turns reaching in, feeling, and describing the tool that they are holding. Can the others guess what the tool is?

Give children objects to match with associated tools: hammer and nails, eggbeater and eggs (hard-boil to prevent breaking), can opener and can, screwdriver and screws. They match corresponding pairs and place on trays together.

With adult supervision, children hammer nails into a piece of plywood so the nail heads stick up. They then stretch rubber bands of different colors around nails to make creative designs.

 "Woodchuck"

 Play "Hot Potato," passing tools as music plays. When music stops, child with tool identifies it and demonstrates how to use it.

Good Wood Bear, by Bijou Le Tord

"Who Built the Ark?" Raffi, More Singable Songs

"Doing What You're Doing— Work and Machines," Science, Unit 2, Scholastic

---

FRIDAY

Discuss safety rules that should be followed when using tools such as hammers, saws, and rakes. Why are these possibly dangerous? Why do construction workers wear hardhats?

Have children line up real tools from smallest to largest, longest to shortest, lightest to heaviest, and oldest to newest.

With adult supervision, children practice safety rules as they build wooden boats from wood scraps with carpenter tools and wood glue. Paint boats bright colors.

 "Carpenter"

 "Wheelbarrow." Child takes partner's feet, and partner walks on hands, making a wheelbarrow. Switch positions and repeat.

 "Pound Goes the Hammer"

The Toolbox, by Anne and Harlow Rockwell

Machines, by Anne and Harlow Rockwell

"Swing, Sway, Twist and Stretch," Hap Palmer, Walter the Waltzing Worm

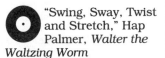

JULY: WEEK 1
Stars and Stripes

	Thinking and Talking	Learning by Doing	Crafts and Creations	Songs and Games	Recommended Resources
MONDAY	Ask children if they know which holiday will be celebrated this week and why we celebrate it. Discuss the typical things people do on the 4th of July. What are fireworks? firecrackers? Discuss safety practices for these items.	Line children up in a parade line. Identify who is the first, second, third, last. Shuffle children and repeat questions. Line children up from oldest to youngest and from youngest to oldest, with each child saying his or her age.	Children make pictures of fireworks at night by drawing multicolored fireworks with wax crayons on drawing paper. They then paint over the paper with thin black tempera paint to create a night sky.	 "I Asked My Mother"  "Little Liza Jane"	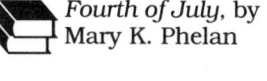 *Fourth of July,* by Mary K. Phelan 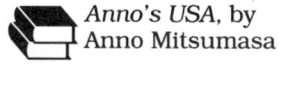 *Anno's USA,* by Anno Mitsumasa 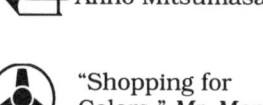 "Shopping for Colors," *Mr. Men and Little Miss Series,* SVE
TUESDAY	Show children a real U.S. flag. Talk about stars and stripes and their meaning. Show pictures of flags from other countries, and have children identify the colors and shapes they see. 	Give children beans, paper plates, foil pie tins, toilet paper rolls, oatmeal cartons, pop bottle tops, paper plates, rubber bands, paper fasteners, wood sticks, yarn, glue, scissors, sandpaper, and tape. Each child constructs the instrument of his or her choice. March around the room, or outside, like a marching band.	Give each child a blue square and strips of red and white construction paper to paste on a sheet of flag-shaped paper. They then paste gold star stickers on the blue background and attach to a dowel or stick to make a U.S. flag. Encourage the children to work from top to bottom and from left to right.	 Give each child a rhythm instrument, and line them up in a parade line. Play marching music and have children march and play their instruments. Have them march and play without music.  "A Rocket in My Pocket"	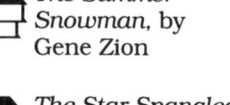 *The Summer Snowman,* by Gene Zion 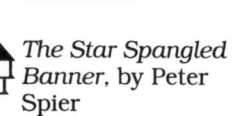 *The Star Spangled Banner,* by Peter Spier 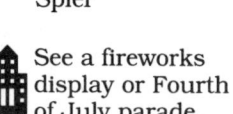 See a fireworks display or Fourth of July parade.

WEDNESDAY

Talk about the United States as a country. Ask children to identify their nationality. Ask, What is the best thing about your country? What would you like to change about your country? Has anyone visited (or lived in) another country? What languages do people from other countries speak? How are things different in other countries?

Take the children outside with a watermelon. Take turns picking it up. Is it heavy? Slice it open. What colors do we see? Give each child a slice. Each child counts the number of seeds in his or her slice. Have a seed-spitting contest.

Discuss the words to the song "America the Beautiful." Children draw a scene reflecting these words, using wet chalk on paper.

 "America the Beautiful"

 "Tomorrow's the Fair"

 "Fireflies"

 Henry's Fourth of July, by Holly Keller

 "Parade of Color," Hap Palmer, *Learning Basic Skills Through Music, Vol. II*

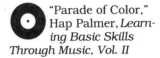 Watch a marching band.

THURSDAY

Show children a picture of a parade. Ask the children to identify what the people are doing and the types of noises we hear in a parade. Take turns imitating some of the noises that people make in a parade. Talk about what we see, hear, and smell at a carnival. What can we taste at a carnival?

Create rhythmic patterns using body parts. Children listen to and repeat them. For example: clap, clap, clap, stomp or tap head, tap head, slap knees, slap knees. Children may wish to take turns leading classmates in rhythmic repetitions.

Children make firecrackers by wrapping a toilet-tissue roll with a rectangular piece of tissue paper, tying ribbons at both ends. Decorate with star stickers.

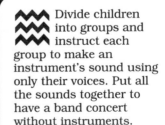

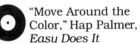 Children make different firecracker noises with their hands and voices: a loud bang, a soft pop, a slow sizzle, and so on.

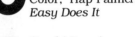 "When Johnny Comes Marching Home"

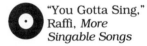 "Move Around the Color," Hap Palmer, *Easy Does It*

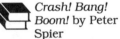 *Crash! Bang! Boom!* by Peter Spier

"You Gotta Sing," Raffi, *More Singable Songs*

FRIDAY

Review the various holidays we celebrate throughout the year and their associated traditions. Have each child name his or her favorite holiday and explain why.

 Children make *Fourth of July Fruit Cups*, using blueberries, bananas, and strawberries—or other red, white, and blue fruits.

 Have children draw a triangle on a piece of paper. Turn paper so base is at the top and paint with thick *Snow Paint* tinted pink to make cotton candy.

Divide children into groups and instruct each group to make an instrument's sound using only their voices. Put all the sounds together to have a band concert without instruments.

 "Oh Dear, What Can the Matter Be?"

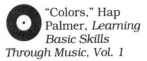 "America the Beautiful," *Mr. Know-It-Owl's Letters, Colors and Ducks*, Kimbo

Henrietta's Fourth of July, by Syd Hoff

 "Colors," Hap Palmer, *Learning Basic Skills Through Music, Vol. 1*

JULY: WEEK 2
Splish, Splash!

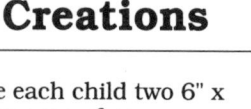

	Thinking and Talking	Learning by Doing	Crafts and Creations	Songs and Games	Recommended Resources
MONDAY	Where do we find water? Make a picture chart of various places where we find water: rain, snow, rivers, sea, faucets, foods. Discuss water pollution. Why must we keep our waters clean?	Children grow sweet potatoes by poking toothpicks into a sweet potato and placing it, narrow end down, into a glass of water. Keep in sunlight, adding water as needed, and watch it sprout. Compare it to a potato that has not been kept in water. Discuss elements that plants need to grow.	Give each child two 6" x 6" squares of paper. Children fold one in half diagonally, open and cut along fold to make two triangular sails. Fold other piece in half vertically and cut along fold to make two 3" x 6" rectangles. Paste onto paper to make sailboats. Paint ocean with roll-on deodorant bottles or shoe polish bottles filled with weak blue tempera paint.	"Pitter-pat" "Freeze." Children move around the room freely while the teacher beats a drum. When the beating stops and the teacher says "freeze," the children stop instantly in whatever position they find themselves in and hold until the drumbeat resumes.	*Water Is Wet*, by Sally Cartwright "Robin in the Rain" and "Down by the Bay," Raffi, *Singable Songs for the Very Young* Go to a lake and watch the various water sports in action. Enlist chaperones and take the class swimming.
TUESDAY	Discuss the many uses of water: cooking, washing, drinking, putting out fires, making things grow. Ask the children to identify things that live in water.	Children free-explore with water and funnels, spoons, cups, colanders, sponges. Add *bubble solution* to water. Bend wire into various shapes for bubble wands. Can you blow a square bubble? Supply buckets of water and large paintbrushes so children can role play painters and "paint" playground equipment.	Cut sponges into summertime shapes, such as seashells, sailboats, flowers, and butterflies. Children dip in tempera paint and make prints on paper.	"The Sea" Children practice swim strokes in the air to music: breaststroke, crawl, backstroke, dog paddle, and floating.	*Rain, Drop, Splash*, by Alvin Tresselt "Water Is in the Air," *Slim Goodbody's World of Weather and Climate*, SVE Ride on a ferryboat or passenger boat.

WEDNESDAY	Observe a transparent container of water. What is water like? Is it heavy? How does it smell? How does it taste? How does it feel? How does it move? Is the water from the faucet different from the water in a lake? Why?	Set out large tub of water. Put a large paper boat on the water. Does it float? Tear the paper into sections and roll into tiny balls. Do these float? Put a little ball of clay on the water. Does it sink or float? Mold clay into a boat. Does it sink or float? Repeat with metal ball and toy metal boat. How can boats be made of metal?	Make *playdough* with the children. Give each child a piece to model and paint after it's dry. Ask the children what happened to the water in the playdough?	"Rain on the Green Grass" "It's Raining, It's Pouring" "Little Drops of Water" 	"Hot Hippo," Weston Woods *Mud, Mud, Mud,* by Leonore Klein *If All the Seas Were One Sea,* by Janina Domanska
THURSDAY	Ask children if water can be found in different forms. Discuss freezing and melting of water. Can water disappear? Where does water go when it evaporates? 	Children explore combining water and various substances—oil, sugar, salt, detergent, sand, dirt, and vinegar. What happens with each? Have children tap on and blow into bottles filled with different amounts of water and discover the differences in the sounds they produce.	Outside, make mud in large container. Children dip feet in mud and make footprints on long sheet of butcher paper. (For easy clean up, have dishpans of soapy water and towels at end of paper.) Dip each child's hands in mud and make handprints on paper with special verse for parents ("Handprints").	Children bring swimsuits to school and play outside in a sprinkler. "A Sailor Went to Sea, Sea, Sea"	*Dawn,* by Molly Bang 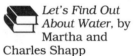 *Let's Find Out About Water,* by Martha and Charles Shapp "Rowing," Preschool Fitness
FRIDAY	Discuss ways we can have fun with water. How many water sports can the children name: swimming, sailing, windsurfing, fishing, water skiing, canoeing, kayaking, surfing, boating, inner-tubing. Children identify ways to travel on water and sort pictures of vehicles that go on water and those that travel on land.	 Children shuck *Corn on the Cob.* Boil in water and serve with butter for a snack.	Give each child an egg carton that has several sections filled with water. Add a few drops of food coloring to some sections. Provide an eyedropper and heavy-duty paper towel so each child can experiment mixing the colors. The colors blend on the paper towel to create beautiful designs.	 Play "Leapfrog." Children line up one behind the other in a squatting position. The last child in line jumps over each "frog" in front of him or her, placing his or her hands on the back of the child and jumping over with one big "leap." "Rain, Rain, Go Away"	*Harry by the Sea,* by Gene Zion *Hot As an Ice Cube,* by Philip Balestrino "Jumping Frog," Hap Palmer, *Pretend* "Plop, Bubble, Fizz," *Science, Unit 2,* Scholastic

JULY: WEEK 3
A, B, C, D, ...

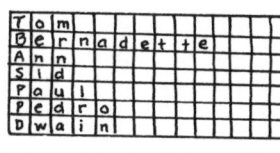

	Thinking and Talking	Learning by Doing	Crafts and Creations	Songs and Games	Recommended Resources
MONDAY	Discuss the importance of putting words and sentences in proper sequence in order to convey ideas correctly. Say a sentence and have the children identify if it is scrambled or sensible. • I washed my car with soap. • I washed my soap with car. • Put the spoon in the drawer. • Put the drawer in the spoon.	As each child says his or her first and last name, write on graph paper to make a name graph. Count letters in each child's name. Who has the longest name? The shortest name? Do any children have the same name? Are they spelled the same? 	Children cover fingerpaint paper with shaving cream, making various designs with their hands. They then write their names (or the first letter of their names) using their finger as a "pencil." (Shaving cream can be tinted with powdered tempera paint.)	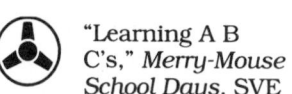 "A, B, C Song" 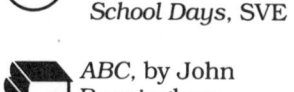 "Have You Ever Seen?" 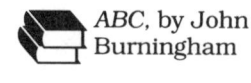 Scatter alphabet cards on floor. Each child selects a letter and stands by it. Give children directions such as jump over letter, run around letter, sit in letter.	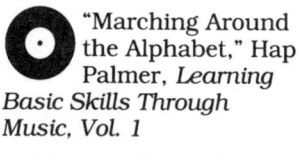 A, B, See, by Tana Hoban "Learning A B C's," Merry-Mouse School Days, SVE ABC, by John Burningham
TUESDAY	Discuss the concept that words can be spoken as well as written. Where do we hear words? Where do we see written words? Show examples of written words: newspapers, magazines, books, signs, labels, greeting cards. 	Help children type their names on a word processor or typewriter. (Enlist help of older student or adult volunteer.) Children draw self-portraits under their names. Compare with self-portraits of September, Week 2. Children write their names at bottom of page.	Children bring a white cotton T-shirt to school and use fabric markers to write their names or initials and draw various designs to decorate.	 "Somebody Loves You" 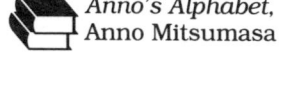 Teach the children to say "I love you" in sign language.  "Days of Week" 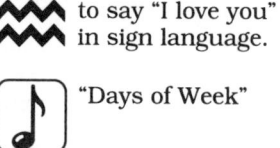 I LOVE YOU	 Anno's Alphabet, Anno Mitsumasa "Marching Around the Alphabet," Hap Palmer, Learning Basic Skills Through Music, Vol. 1 Tour the public library; have librarian read stories to the class.

WEDNESDAY	Show the class a chart of the letters of the alphabet. Count how many there are. Recite or sing them together. Can anyone identify some of the letters? What letter does the name of each child begin with?	To illustrate that everything has a name, label many items in the classroom. Give each child a word card and have them find labeled object that matches card. Give children cardboard circles (pizza forms work well) with letters around edge, and clothespins with a letter on each. Children clip clothespins onto matching letters.	Children make "Personalized Pretzels" in the shape of their initial and eat for snack. 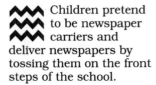	"Who Feels Happy?" 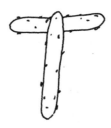 Children pretend to be newspaper carriers and deliver newspapers by tossing them on the front steps of the school.	*Action Alphabet*, by Marty Newmeier and Byron Glaser *Hosie's Alphabet*, by Leonard Baskin "Something That Begins Like" and "Words on the Board," Hap Palmer, *Learning Basic Skills Through Music, Vol. II*

THURSDAY	Discuss what is fun about reading and hearing stories. Let each child name his or her favorite story. Is writing fun? Why do people need to learn how to write? Demonstrate a typewriter or word processor.	Children take turns writing their names with index finger in a tray of wet sand.
		 Write each child's name in large letters on a piece of paper. Child squeezes glue along letters (less mature children may put glue over the first letter only) and then sprinkles with dry sand.
			Children make a "sounds collage" by cutting and pasting pictures that begin with the same sounds as their names. Help each child find a picture that has the same beginning sound as his or her name. Do different names begin with the same sounds?	Pin a letter on the front of each child and line up the class in alphabetical order. Children march around the room to music to create an alphabet parade. "Solomon Grundy"	*On Market Street*, by Arnold Lobel
					  A-B-C-ing, by Janet Beller
					  Have an author or illustrator visit the classroom.

FRIDAY	Discuss authors and what they do. Ask the children if they know what an illustrator does. What tools does a writer use? An illustrator? 	Each child can be an author and an illustrator. Children create and dictate stories for teacher to print on plain paper stapled together to make a small storybook. Children draw illustrations for each page with crayons or colored pencils.	Give each child a 2-dimensional outline of the first letter of his or her name. Children tear or cut wallpaper into small scraps and paste onto letter to make "calico letters." 	Children try to form alphabet letters using their bodies. Show a large alphabet card and have children arrange their limbs and torsos to imitate the letter. See how long children can balance and hold various positions. "Hey Lolly, Lolly"	*The Most Amazing Hide and Seek Alphabet Book*, by Robert Crowther *Alfred's Alphabet Walk*, by Victoria Chess  "Alphabet Match-Up," *Mr. Men and Little Miss Discover Colors, Shapes and the Alphabet*, SVE

JULY: WEEK 4
Real Dragons

SKILLS TO INTRODUCE

- Discriminate between living and nonliving things (S)
- Demonstrate awareness of reproduction (S)
- Identify and name animals (S)
- Select and name opposites (LA)
- Recall details from a story (LA)
- Follow maze and connect dot-to-dot patterns (LA)
- Sort and classify objects into sets (M)
- Recognize numerals: 1, 2, 3, 4, 5, . . . (M)
- Demonstrate understanding of concepts: near and far, loud and soft, fast and slow, long and short, high and low (Mu)
- Work with classmates on group art projects (A)
- Imitate various ways of walking (PE)

	Thinking and Talking	Learning by Doing	Crafts and Creations	Songs and Games	Recommended Resources
M O N D A Y	Read a dragon story and discuss dragons. Did dragons ever exist? Were there ever any animals that lived that looked like dragons? Are dinosaurs living today? Were dinosaurs real? What do we know about dinosaurs? Read a nonfiction book and have children recall and state facts from it.	Give children small rubber dinosaurs to sort into sets. First sort the same kinds; then sort into groups by color and by size. Count how many are in each set. 	Children color and cut out a two-piece head and jaw of a Tyrannosaurus Rex *("Tyrannosaurus Rex Puppet")*. Join with a paper fastener so his mouth can open and close.	"Dragon Hunt" "Fee, Fie, Foe, Fum"	*There's No Such Thing as a Dragon*, by Jack Kent *The Once-Upon-a-Time Dragon*, by Jack Kent "Listen and Do," Hap Palmer, *Learning Basic Skills Through Music, Vol IV*
T U E S D A Y	How were dinosaurs born? What other animals are hatched from eggs? What did the dinosaur's world look like? Ask children to finish statements such as • The Tyrannosaurus Rex was not friendly; he was ___. (fierce) • The Brontosaurus was not small; he was ___. (big, huge) • The Triceratops was not heavy; he was ___. (light)	Draw and cut out dinosaur cards with numbers written on them *("Dinosaur and Leaves Pattern")*. Hide the cards throughout the room. Children go on a dinosaur hunt. They identify the numbers they "caught." They can also "feed" each dinosaur by placing the proper number of small cut-out leaves on each card.	Form chicken wire into shape of Brontosaurus. With strips of paper and papier-mâché glue *(Papier Mâché)*, class makes a giant dinosaur. Paint when dry. Each child can make a dinosaur skeleton by bending pipe cleaners into a round head, long body, four legs, and small spikes along spine.	"Don't Let the Dragons Get You" Children move around the room imitating different dinosaurs: lumbering like a Brontosaurus, flying like a Pteranodon, arms up like a Tyrannosaurus, swimming like a Plesiosaur and Mosasaur, and so on.	"Plant-Eating Dinosaurs" and "Meat-Eating Dinosaurs," *When Dinosaurs Lived*, SVE *Dragon ABC Hunt*, by Loreen Leedy *Dinosaurs*, by Gail Gibbons

WEDNESDAY

Discuss the diet of dinosaurs. Which ones ate meat? Which ones ate plants? Show pictures of these two groups of dinosaurs and discuss their physical differences. Sort them into 2 groups. How many dinosaurs can we name? (Brontosaurus, Tyrannosaurus Rex, Brachiosaurus, Trachodon, and Triceratops are a few.)

 Children trace "Dot-to-Dot Stegosaurus." Paint with glue and cover with cornflake "spikes." Draw something for him to eat.

Children paint a large mural of dinosaur-country vegetation, including various trees, plants, and even lakes. Each child draws, colors, cuts out, and pastes a dinosaur onto the mural.

 "A-hunting We Will Go"

 Beat a drum emphasizing different rhythms for the children to move with. Accompany changes in drum rhythm with a story, "Now the dinosaurs are near and we are in danger and must move very fast." "The drum is beating softly; now they are far away and we can walk slowly."

 Emma's Dragon Hunt, by Catherine Stock

 Dinosaur Time, by Peggy Parish

 "Oh Me, Oh My" and "If I Had A Dinosaur," Raffi, *More Singable Songs*

THURSDAY

Show toy or model dinosaurs. Are they alive? What animals live today that look like dinosaurs? Show pictures of lizards, turtles, iguanas. How do we tell whether something is living or is not alive?

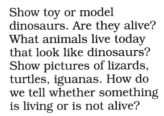 Make a *Dinosaur's Salad* with edible plants.

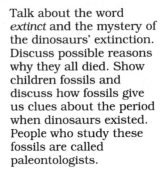

Carve dinosaur footprints of different shapes on bottom of potato halves. Children print footprints (fossils) onto paper.

 "Unfortunately"

 "Dinosaurs"

 Danny and the Dinosaur, by Aliki

 Lyle Finds His Mother, by Bernard Waber

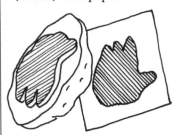 Visit a museum to see dinosaur bones and fossils.

FRIDAY

Talk about the word *extinct* and the mystery of the dinosaurs' extinction. Discuss possible reasons why they all died. Show children fossils and discuss how fossils give us clues about the period when dinosaurs existed. People who study these fossils are called paleontologists.

Talk about the size of dinosaurs. Lay a 70-foot length of string on playground to illustrate length of Brontosaurus. Children lie down in a row, head to toe, on string. The Brontosaurus was longer than how many children?

Children make 3-D dioramas in shoe boxes using sand, rocks, leafy twigs secured with bits of clay, and blades of grass. Place toy dinosaurs inside and let the children dramatize.

Have dinosaur races in which the children walk first on feet with hands on floor, then fly, then crawl on stomachs.

 "Five Huge Dinosaurs"

 Invite a paleontologist or representative from natural history museum to speak to the class.

 "Where the Wild Things Are," Weston Woods

 Where the Wild Things Are, by Maurice Sendak

 Dinosaurs, by Peter Zallinger

AUGUST: WEEK 1
Shapes and More Shapes

	Thinking and Talking	Learning by Doing	Crafts and Creations	Songs and Games	Recommended Resources
MONDAY	Put large group of geometrical objects, flat and 3-D, on floor in front of children. Have the children take turns finding objects that are the same and designating what traits (color, size, shape) make them similar. Arrange shapes to form pictures; children identify object made from the shapes.	Children string beads in various geometrical shapes, copying from pattern cards. Let children invent their own patterns and describe them to classmates.	Give each child a piece of drawing paper with a sandpaper triangle pasted on it. See what each child can create with the triangle, using wet chalk or felt-tip markers. A fish? A house? A boat? A hat? An ice cream cone? A witch?	"Clementine" Introduce "kickball" by having the children take turns kicking the ball and running around the bases.	*Round, Round and Round*, by Tana Hoban "Triangle, Circle and Square" and "One Shape, Three Shapes," Hap Palmer, *Learning Basic Skills Through Music, Vol. II*
TUESDAY	Put 3-D geometrical objects in a box for children to feel without looking. Children take turns identifying shapes by touch. Each child should describe how his or her shape feels.	Children sort attribute blocks by size, color, and shape. Working with a partner, children copy each other's designs and patterns.	Each child draws and cuts out his or her favorite shape to make a shape puppet. Children color the faces and attach them to popsicle sticks or tongue depressors. 	"Here's a Ball" Put different shapes on the floor, one for each child. Each child stands on a shape and follows teacher's directions. "Circles, hop three times." "Squares, stand on one foot for the count of ten." When teacher says "scramble," children run to find a new shape.	*Shapes, Shapes, Shapes*, by Tana Hoban "Shape Search," *Mr. Men and Little Miss Series*, SVE *Shapes to Show*, by Karen Gundersheimer

WEDNESDAY

Show and name some 3-D shapes. Ask the children to point out objects in classroom that have similar shapes. Who can find an object that has the same shape as this cube? Children identify other objects that represent various shapes, such as wheels, windows, doors, signs, and kites.

 Children make *Shape Kabobs* by sticking 1 cheese circle, 1 ham triangle, and 2 pineapple cubes onto a toothpick.

Children paint at easel on paper with negative space stencils of triangles, circles, and squares. See which shape children like to paint best!

 Children move the way they think a shape would: A circle rolls, a square bumps, a triangle slides, an oval rocks, and so on.

 "Clap with Me"

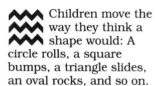 *Shapes,* by John J. Reiss

 Circles, Triangles and Squares, by Tana Hoban

 Visit a city and note the shapes of the buildings.

THURSDAY

Make absurd and true statements about the shape of things and have children decide if the statement is correct.
- Trucks have square wheels.
- A plate is like a circle.
- A baseball is pointed like a kite.

With construction paper, templates, scissors, and crayons, each child traces and cuts out a shape that represents a city building. All buildings can be glued to mural paper to make a city street. Children enjoy adding fringed green rectangle grass, triangle roofs, square chimneys and windows, oval clouds, round sun, and so forth.

 Using cookie cutters, plastic knives, and their hands, children make flat and 3-D shapes from *clay.*

 "Bow Belinda"

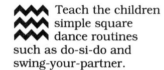 Teach the children simple square dance routines such as do-si-do and swing-your-partner.

 Shapes, by Jan Pienkowski

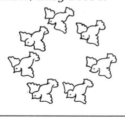 "Birds in the Circle" and "Circle Your Way," Hap Palmer, *Easy Does It*

FRIDAY

Ask children to find body parts using shapes as clues. "Point to a body part that is round like a circle." "Point to something that is small and oval." "What part of your face resembles a triangle?" Show pictures of objects with obvious shapes and have children name the shapes: circular wheels, square windows, triangular ice cream cones, circular clocks.

Give each child four black paper circles, a large rectangular piece of construction paper, a small paper triangle, scissors, and paste. Instruct children to create the vehicles of their choice and paste onto a large sheet of paper. Ask children to point the top, middle, and bottom of their vehicles.

Children make rainbow shapes by painting with watercolors around and around a shape, each time using a new color.

 "Punchinello"

 "This Is the Circle That Makes My Head"

 Take a shape walk around school, searching for square things, round things, and triangular things.

The Town Mouse and the Country Mouse, by Lorinda Bryan Cauley

 "Geometric Shapes," *Beginning Math Concepts, Group 1,* SVE

AUGUST: WEEK 2
Around the Campfire

	Thinking and Talking	Learning by Doing	Crafts and Creations	Songs and Games	Recommended Resources
MONDAY	Set up a tent in the classroom and show pictures of different types of tents and campers. Has anyone ever been camping? Do people live in tents? Discuss tents as temporary and permanent homes. Discuss the sounds you hear at a campground. Are they different from sounds on a city street?	 Children make a *Trail Mix* snack by counting ten of each item and placing all in a plastic sandwich bag. 	Children make a class mural of a forest. They dip small sponges in tempera to make tree leaves and color trees, clouds, and a sun. Crumple small pieces of black paper to make bugs and paste them on the mural. Glue on crushed pieces of tissue paper or small cupcake liners for flowers.	 "In a Cabin" "Cock-a-doodle-doo" "Oh, How Lovely Is the Evening"	*Just Me and My Dad,* by Mercer Mayer "The More We Get Together" and "The Sharing Song," Raffi, *Singable Songs for the Very Young* "Arthur's Teacher Trouble and Arthur goes to Camp," Kimbo
TUESDAY	Discuss where people go camping: in the city? in the country? in the ocean? What kind of weather is best for camping? What time of year do most people prefer to camp? 	Play listening game "I packed my grandma's knapsack and I put in . . ." Finish the sentence with an object to take on a camping trip. Each child repeats the sentence and adds a new item. Add funny as well as realistic items. "I packed my grandma's knapsack and I put in a snake!"	Children collect twigs, pebbles, tiny pine cones, and other small nature objects and stick them into a ball of clay to make a nature sculpture. 	Children practice various kinds of rolling: somersaults, down a hill with arms overhead, back and forth with arms around knees, side to side with arms folded at chest, and so on. "August Heat"	 Visit a forest preserve or state park. *Three Days on a River in a Red Canoe,* by Vera B. Williams *Turtle Tale,* by Frank Asch

WEDNESDAY	Bring a backpack filled with camping items, such as a pocket knife, compass, skillet, and sunglasses. Identify the items and discuss their purpose. Identify the articles of clothing needed for a summer camping trip. What foods should we take? How about soap, toothbrush, and sleeping bag?	Set several camping items on the table. Children close their eyes and along comes a "bear" and snatches an item. Children open their eyes and name what's missing. 	Take children outside, preferably to a scenic area, with paper, crayons, and something hard to draw on. Everyone picks a spot in which to sit and draws a landscape. (Even the younger children can find something to draw: a tree, the sky, the sun.	"She'll Be Coming 'Round the Mountain" "Flashlight Hide-and-Seek." Dim light and give one child a flashlight. "It" counts to ten as the rest of the class hides, then tries to catch someone with the light.	"Remembering a Camping Trip," *Developing Visual Memory,* SVE 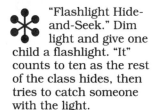 *Camping Out,* by Betsy and Giulio Maestro *Deep in the Forest,* by Brinton Turkle

THURSDAY	Show children a first-aid kit. Discuss the importance of having such a kit when camping and what the various items are needed for. Talk about forest fires and safety rules we should follow on a camping trip. 	Simulate a classroom camping trip by having the children bring sleeping bags (or blankets) and pajamas. They should also bring their favorite "cuddly." Take turns "sleeping" in classroom tent. Without assistance, children change into pajamas, brush teeth, and wash up before bed. Turn out lights and ask "Who's scared?"	Children make ladybugs by painting half a walnut shell red and adding black dots. Commercial wiggle eyes can be glued on for added effect. 	"Playmates" Children put on backpacks and take a hike around the playground or neighborhood, pretending they are hiking in the mountains.	*Pig-Pig Goes to Camp,* by David McPhail "Growing," Hap Palmer, *Learning Basic Skills Through Music, Vol 1* Invite a forest ranger to speak on camping safety.

FRIDAY	Describe situations that might occur on a camping trip and ask children what their reactions would be. "You are wading in a stream and you hear thunder. How would you feel? What would you do?" "You see a deer hiding behind some bushes. What would you do?" "You spot a campfire that was not properly extinguished. What would you do?"	Invite parents for an evening cookout. Take a hike, roast hot dogs and then marshmallows for *S'Mores.* Don't forget to sing campfire songs around the campfire!	Draw large knapsack on mural paper. Children cut out pictures of camping items from catalogues and magazines and glue them in the outline of knapsack. Count together number of items in the knapsack. 	"I Love the Mountains" "Kum Ba Ya" On playground or at park, children collect small sticks. Partners take turns making and copying designs in dirt with stick. Can make designs with feet also.	Go on an overnight camping trip at a local campsite or in one of the parents' yards. *The Hunting Trip,* by Robert Burch *Having a Picnic,* by Sarah Garland "Park Ranger," *People Who Work, Unit 1,* Scholastic

AUGUST: WEEK 3
Money, Money, Money!

	Thinking and Talking	Learning by Doing	Crafts and Creations	Songs and Games	Recommended Resources
MONDAY	Bring coins and dollar bills to share with class. Talk about money. What do we call these coins? What do we use money for? What are these things made of? Together, name different coins and values.	Paste or tape different coin on the outside of several small jars or empty margarine tubs. Give children a cup full of various coins to separate into matching sets. Count together the number of coins in each set.	Children make coin rubbings by putting coins under typing paper and gently rubbing with side of peeled crayon. 	"Hot Cross Buns" "Make New Friends" "A Young Lady of Lynn"	*The Five Pennies,* by Barbara Brenner "Remembering a Supermarket," *Developing Visual Memory,* SVE "Change," Hap Palmer, *Getting to Know Myself*
TUESDAY	Talk about the kinds of things we buy with money. Ask if anyone has ever purchased an item with money. What things can't we buy with money? (health, friendship, love) 	Give children a worksheet with the outline of various coins traced in each row *("Counting Coins").* Children place real coins on top of each outline. Count them together and write or paste numeral indicating how many are in each row.	Children trace around large coins on construction paper, then cut circles out and paste them together on construction paper to make a caterpillar. They draw the face with crayons and add pipe cleaner pieces for antennae. Count together number of circles in each caterpillar.	Place coins inside different containers such as jars, plastic tubs, paper sacks, cardboard boxes, match boxes, and plastic bags. Give each child a container to shake and have a money band. "Spin a Coin"	*Alexander, Who Used to Be Rich Last Sunday,* by Judith Viorst *Count and See,* by Tana Hoban "Rumpelstiltskin," *Children's Stories,* SVE

WEDNESDAY	Ask questions such as, How do people get money? What kind of work do your parents do to receive money? Who are workers in our community who earn money for doing a job? Discuss reasons why people work. What are some jobs we do without payment? Where do people work? Name stores and their functions.	Give each child a handful of coins and ask them to hold up the newest coin, the oldest coin, the biggest coin, the shiniest coin, and the smallest coin. Drop copper pennies into 1 cup vinegar with 1/2 tablespoon salt. Stir and watch as solution cleans pennies.	Children make banks from empty bandage boxes, tea tins, or margarine tubs. Help children cover with adhesive paper or decorate with stickers. Put a penny in each child's bank to start their savings. Point out one penny for each bank is 1-to-1 correspondence.	"One for the Money"
				
				  "See-Saw Margery Daw"
				
				 Have a penny race. Give each child a penny to push along a 2-yard track with nose. See who can toss a penny the farthest and who can roll a penny.
					Visit a bank.
					
					  The Money Book, by Joan W. German

THURSDAY	Show pictures of objects cut from catalogues and ask the children to identify which items are expensive and which cost a small amount of money. If you had a lot of money, what would you like to buy? Which one is the *most* expensive?

Take children to store to buy lemons, sugar, and paper cups. Class uses measuring cups and spoons to make *Old-fashioned Lemonade* and sets up a lemonade stand. Help children figure out how much money to charge for lemonade. Invite parents and friends to buy lemonade. Together, count the money collected and decide if the class made a "profit."

Children draw or paint a picture of what they would buy if they had "a million dollars"!

Take turns tossing pennies into a "wishing well" made from a round ice cream carton.

 "To Market"

 Bravo, Ernest and Celestine! by Gabrielle Vincent

 26 Letters and 99 Cents, by Tana Hoban

 "Lucky Numbers," *Learning Basic Skills Through Music, Vol 2*

FRIDAY

Bring items such as a cash register, money tray, billfold, money belt, piggy bank, and coin purse to share with the children. What are these items for? Show a picture of a bank and talk about saving money.

Children look through catalogues or magazines and cut out something they would like to buy if they had "a lot of money." They then paste them together on a large piece of butcher paper to make a "What I'd buy" collage. Did any children select the same item?

Children make prints from lemon halves dipped in different colors of tempera paint. (Slice lemons in half and let dry overnight for best results.)

 "Simple Simon"

"Hippety-Hop to the Barber Shop"

Child places penny on top of head and tries to walk across room without dropping it. Child can then put a penny on back of each hand and walk across room. Try these stunts on balance beam.

 Fox and Heggie, by Sandra Guzza

 Is It Larger? Is It Smaller? by Tana Hoban

 Go to a store and observe a clerk using a cash register.

AUGUST: WEEK 4
Huff and Puff

	Thinking and Talking	Learning by Doing	Crafts and Creations	Songs and Games	Recommended Resources
MONDAY	Blow up a balloon and ask the children why the balloon got bigger. Talk about what air is and where we find it. Fill balloons with air, with water, and with sand. Children compare weight and size of balloons, identifying the biggest, heaviest, smallest, and lightest.	Put a candle inside a glass jar and light the candle. What happens if you put the lid on the jar? Repeat experiment with a large jar and a small jar and observe which candle goes out first. Discuss why the flame went out.	Make bubble prints by adding a bit of tempera paint to equal parts of water and liquid detergent. Children use straw to blow bubbles into a jar of solution sitting on a piece of paper. As bubbles overflow, they will land on the paper, burst, and leave colored prints.	♪ "A-tisket, A-tasket" 〰 Bring a large sheet or parachute to class. Everyone holds on as they walk in a circle, run, and shake the parachute. On the count of 3, everyone raises their arms (holding the parachute) up in the air. Take turns running under the parachute.	📚 *Joseph Jacob's "The Story of the Three Little Pigs,"* illustrated by Lorinda Bryan Cauley 📚 *A Children's Museum Activity Book: Bubbles,* by Bernie Zubrowski ◉ Brother to the Wind, Weston Woods
TUESDAY	With children observing, let air from a filled balloon empty into a plastic sack and close sack to trap the air. Put neck of a filled balloon next to a candle flame and let the air blow the candle out. What happened? Discuss how we know that air exists. Can we see air? Feel it? Taste it? Smell it? Hear it?	Give children various cutouts of objects, such as trees, insects, birds, clouds, flowers, pets, balloons, kites, houses, and a sun. Children place these objects on the flannelboard to make a scene. Ask children to tell where the objects are placed: "the flowers are beside the house," "the kite is stuck in the tree," and so on.	Give each child a blown-up balloon, pieces of string or yarn, and a dish filled with tinted glue. Children dip string into glue and wrap around the balloon. When glue dries, pop the balloon. The result is an interesting sculpture. 	〰 Partners roll a Ping-Pong ball back and forth across a table by blowing it—no hands! Try this with a tennis ball and golf ball. ✿ "Five Birthday Candles" 	📚 *Air Is All Around You,* by Franklyn M. Branley ◉ "Whirling Winds," *Slim Goodbody's World of Weather and Climate,* SVE ⦿ "Sammy," Hap Palmer, *Getting to Know Myself*

WEDNESDAY

Bring a fan to school and tie strips of crepe paper to outer frame. Turn on fan and watch what happens to the paper strips. What can air do? Can it move things? Talk about things that air (wind) can move.

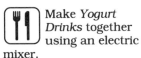 Give children a worksheet of an unfinished picture of a birthday cake *(Unfinished Birthday Cake)*. Children complete the picture by drawing correct number of candles for their age. How old are you? Children write their names under their cake.

Children make streamers by cutting long strips of crepe paper and attaching them to popsicle sticks with staples or glue. Children take streamers outside and run around the playground. What happens to the streamers when the children stand still?

 Divide class into two groups and give each group a balloon. See which group can keep the balloon in the air the longest. Give each child a balloon to try to blow up and keep in the air with hands and feet. Take everyone outside with shoes and socks off for a water balloon toss.

 "Blow a Balloon"

 The Day the Hurricane Happened, by Lonzo Anderson

Watch a hot-air balloon take off and land.

Home in the Sky, by Jeannie Baker

THURSDAY

Talk about the many ways air can help us and about machines that use air to help us such as hair dryers, fans, windmills, electric mixers, clothes dryers, sailboats, and air conditioners. What vehicles go in the air?

 Make *Yogurt Drinks* together using an electric mixer. Where do the bubbles in the liquid come from?

Children make hot air balloons by coloring coffee filters with bright-colored felt-tip markers and dipping in water. They punch two holes in a square basket cut from brown construction paper and connect with yarn to dried filter "balloon." Hang balloons from ceiling.

 Make "popcorn" with the parachute by putting two or three balls on it and shaking up and down with arms.

With everyone holding on, lift the parachute up high in the air, bring down quickly and sit on the edge to catch air in the middle.

 "Up a Step"

 The Red Balloon, by Albert Lamorisse

 "Shake My Sillies Out," Raffi, *More Singable Songs*

 "The Wind and the Sun," *Aesop's Famous Fables*, SVE

Hot-Air Henry, by Mary Calhoun

FRIDAY

Discuss air pollution. Is air the same in the city as in the countryside? Talk about ways we can keep our air and our environment cleaner.

Children make pinwheels from square piece of paper, cutting diagonally from each corner to center, and folding corners to center *("Pinwheel")*. They tack pinwheel to pencil eraser. Blow and watch pinwheel move.

Give each child an empty walnut shell, a tiny ball of clay, a toothpick, and a piece of white paper. Children assemble to make sailboats and float in laundry tubs filled with water. Children can have races, blowing their boats across the water.

 "Michael Finnegan"

Children listen and relax or move freely to various types of music. Celebrate end of school year with a birthday party (or, as in *Alice in Wonderland*, an *un*birthday party). Each child gets a cupcake with a candle to blow out. Sing "Happy Birthday" to everyone. Everyone blows a kiss to say goodbye!

Whistle for Willie, by Ezra Jack Keats

"Put Your Hands Up in the Air," Hap Palmer, *Learning Basic Skills Through Music, Vol 1*

 A clown or other special visitor comes to blow up helium balloons and give to the children.

Games for Growing

The following games are great for filling those periods between activities. These games can be enjoyed any time of the day and any day of the year. On p.126 is an index of the games described in the *Year-Round Calendar*.

Hotter . . . Colder: An object is hidden in the room while one student is outside. When the student returns, he or she attempts to find the object as the class gives the clues "hotter, hotter, hotter" when the child is near the object, and "colder, colder, colder" when the child is far from the object.

How Many Times: While the teacher tells a simple story, the children listen and count silently how many times the teacher says a certain word, such as *dog* or *cookie*. The children may wish to hold their fingers under the table to help them count. At the end of the story, the teacher checks to see how many children counted the correct number of times the word was used in the story.

I See Something: The teacher describes something in the classroom and the children try to guess what the object is by the description. For example: "I see something red. It is bigger than my hand. It is round and smooth. We use it on the playground." ("That's correct: a ball.")

I Went to the Store: The teacher says, "I went to the store and I bought some bananas." A student repeats the sentence and adds an item, "I went to the store and I bought some bananas and a loaf of bread." Repeat around the group, with each child recalling all previous items and adding a new one. How many can be repeated in sequence?

Listen and Line Up: The teacher calls students to line up or to go to their seats by categories: "Everyone who is wearing the color green can get in line" or "All boys with blue tennis shoes can sit down" or "Everyone who rode the school bus today can sit in the circle."

Pass the Beanbag: Children pass the beanbag from child to child as a record plays. When the record stops, the child holding the beanbag performs a motion, song, rhyme, or movement. The others can imitate or join in.

Pet Puppet: Keep your classroom "pet" in a box and bring it out to fill a few minutes and reinforce some concepts each week. Let the puppet tell a poem, give directions, ask riddles, call out addresses of children to come to lunch, spell names of children to go outside, and ask children to put toys away!

Repeating Rhythms: The teacher demonstrates a rhythm by clapping, tapping, and slapping (for example, clap hands, clap hands, tap head, slap the table). The children watch and repeat the rhythmic activity when the teacher says, "Go."

Shopping Sack: The teacher takes a shopping sack or a large purse and fills the sack with objects, naming each object as it is put in the sack. The students are then asked to recall which items were placed in the sack. Can the class remember all of them?

Simon Says: The teacher gives a command such as "Simon says put your hands on your head" or "Simon says stand up." The teacher will try to "trick" the children by giving a command without beginning it by saying "Simon says." A child who does an action that Simon did not say is eliminated, or the teacher can simply say, "Oh, I tricked Billy, Susie, and Shawn!"

Surprise of the Day: Each day place something in a "feely" box or sack. The children take turns reaching in and feeling to guess the hidden item. Then they examine the object and discuss its use.

Telephone: The teacher whispers something in a child's ear. The child whispers the message to the next child. The message passes from child to child, and the last child repeats the message aloud.

Additional games can be found throughout *Every Day in Every Way: A Year-Round Calendar of Preschool Learning Challenges.*

Sources of Materials for Early–Childhood Programs

Books

Many of the books recommended in the *Year-Round Calendar* can be borrowed from your local library. (An increasing number of school and public libraries have toy-lending libraries, too.) Your librarian is also an outstanding source of information about ordering materials. To see if a book is still in print (and thus available from the publisher), look it up at the library in the current edition of *Children's Books in Print* or *Books in Print* (both published by R. R. Bowker). If any of the books listed in the *Year-Round Calendar* are not available from your local library or bookstore, they can be ordered directly from the publisher or from a distributor (you may be eligible for a discount if you order a shipment from a distributor). The following are just two of several distributors of books for children. Write to them for more information.

Brodart
500 Arch Street
Williamsport, PA 17705

Baker and Taylor
Attn: Direction of Marketing, School Libraries
652 East Main Street
Bridgewater, NJ 08807

The following periodicals and organizations review of the most recent children's books:

Association for Childhood Education International
11141 Georgia Avenue, Suite 200
Wheaton, MD 20902

Booklist
American Library Association
50 East Huron
Chicago, IL 60611

R. R. Bowker
245 West 17th Street
New York, NY 10011

National Association for the Education of Young Children
1834 Connecticut Avenue NW
Washington, DC 20009

School Library Journal
249 West 17th Street
New York, NY 10011

Records

The following records contain selections recommended in the *Year-Round Calendar*. They are current favorites in early childhood programs. If these records are not available at local record stores, they may be ordered from the record company or from Educational Record Center, Building 400, Suite 400, 1575 Northside Drive NW, Atlanta, GA 30318; (404) 352-8282.

Single-Artist Records

Ella Jenkins (Folkways Records, Birchtree Group, 180 Alexander St., Princeton, NJ 08540)

And One and Two
Growing Up with Ella Jenkins
You'll Sing a Song

Alan Mills (Folkways Records, Birchtree Group, 180 Alexander St., Princeton, NJ 08540)

14 Numbers, Letters and Animal Sounds

Hap Palmer (Educational Activities, P.O. Box 392, Freeport, NY 11520)

Easy Does It
Getting to Know Myself
Learning Basic Skills Through Music: Health and Safety
Learning Basic Skills Through Music: Vocabulary
Learning Basic Skills Through Music: Volume I
Learning Basic Skills Through Music: Volume II
Pretend
Walter the Waltzing Worm

Raffi (Kimbo, P.O. Box 477F, Long Branch, NJ 07740)

More Singable Songs
Raffi's Christmas
Singable Songs for the Very Young

Nancy Raven (Pacific Cascade Records, 47534 McKenzie Hwy., Vida, OR 97488)

Hop, Skip and Sing

Rosenshontz (RS Records, Box 651, Brattleboro, VT 05301)

Share It!
Tickles You!

Multiartist Records

Disney's Children's Favorites (Disneyland/Vista Records and Tapes, 350 South Buena Vista Street, Burbank, CA 91521)

Preschool Fitness (Melody House, 819 NW 92nd Street, Oklahoma City, OK 73114)

Tempo for Tots (Melody House, 819 NW 92nd Street, Oklahoma City, OK 73114)

Classical Corner

These classics are available in many versions.

Nutcracker Suite
Peter and the Wolf
Sleeping Beauty
Swan Lake

Filmstrips and Videos

The following audio-visual selections are recommended in the *Year-Round Calendar*. All entries are filmstrips unless otherwise noted. Scholastic's filmstrips come in sets; the remaining filmstrips can be ordered by individual titles.

Encyclopedia Britannica (425 North Michigan Avenue, Chicago, IL 60611; filmstrips may be ordered by individual titles)

Color, Size and Shape

What Do You See? Color!
What Do You See? Shapes!

Experiences in Perceptual Growth

Lions Don't Always Roar
Squish and Prickles

Learning About Animals

Mother Rabbit and Her Family

Myself and Me

What Do I Look Like?

What Is It?

Let's Guess: What Person Is It?
Let's Guess: What Plant Is It?

Kimbo Educational (P.O. Box 477F, Long Branch, NJ 07740)

Arthur's Teacher Trouble and Arthur Goes
  to Camp (video)
Corduroy
Mr. Know-It-Owl's Letters, Colors, and
  Ducks
Nimble Numbers (video)

The Polished Apple (3742 Seahorn Drive, Malibu, CA 90265)

The Snacking Mouse
The Snacking Mouse Goes to School
Nutrition for Children

Scholastic (2931 McCarty Street, Jefferson City, MO 65102; filmstrips must be ordered in sets)

Beginning Concepts, Unit 1

Boxes Clocks Building Blocks
Bumpy Lumpy
Count See One Two Three
Red Blue Yellow Too
Short Tall Large Small

Beginning Concepts, Unit 2

Day Night Heavy Light
Ears Nose Fingers Toes
In Out Roundabout
Kitten Pup Grows Up
Slow Fast First Last

Five Children

Cowboy
Fisherman's Son
Happy Birthday Howard
Mira, Mira Marisol
Sara's Letter

Five Families

Chinatown
Circus Family
Piñata
Together
Yah-a-Tay

Kindle I: Who Am I?

All Kinds of Feelings
Do You Believe in Wishes
The Joy of Being You
Nothing Is Something to Do
People Packages

Kindle III: Getting Along

I Don't Care Anyhow
It's Mine
Smiles Don't Just Happen
Sticks and Stones
Will You Be My Friend?

People Who Work, Unit 1

Bake a Batch of Bread—Baker
Park Ranger—Park Ranger
Pick a Pattern Pick a Patch—Quiltmaker
Say Ah—Pediatrician
Stitch and Stuff—Toy Factory

People Who Work, Unit 2

Click—Photographer
Follow the Architect's Plan—Architect
Jet Pilot—Pilot
On Rainbow Farm—Farm Family
Pets for Sale—Pet Store Owner

Science, Unit 1

Bones Wings Teeth and Things—Structure
  of Plants and Animals
Hide and Seek—Adaptation
Sharing and Caring—Plants, Animals, and
  Us
Something Old Something New—Birth, Life
  and Death
Whales Snails Ants and Plants—Plants and
  Animals

Science, Unit 2

The Changing Earth and Sky—The Earth
  and Our Relationship to It
Doing What You're Doing—Work and
  Machines
Down to Earth—The Earth and Our
  Relationship to It
Plop Bubble Fizz—Solids, Liquids, and
  Gases
What's Going On?—Energy

SVE (1345 Diversey Parkway, Chicago, IL
60614; filmstrips may be orderd by
individual titles)

Aesop's Famous Fables

The Wind and the Sun
Animals in Verse (video)

Baby Animals in Rhyme and Song

Baby Pet Animals in Rhyme and Song
Baby Zoo Animals in Rhyme and Song

Beginning Math Concepts, Group 1

Geometric Shapes

The Changing Seasons

Autumn in My Neighborhood
The Birds Know It's Spring

Children's Stories

Rumpelstiltskin

Developing Visual Memory

Remembering a Camping Trip
Remembering a Supermarket
Remembering a Zoo

Discovering Magnets and Electricity

Discovering Magnets

Fall Holiday Celebrations

Squanto and the First Thanksgiving

*Fran Allison's Autumn Tales of Winnie the
Witch*

Winnie the Witch and the Frightened Ghost
Hanukkah Hotcakes

Health Adventures of the Lollipop Dragon

Food and Growth

Holiday Adventures of the Lollipop Dragon

The Big Easter Egg Hunt
Lollipop Dragon's First Halloween
Lollipop Dragon Helps Santa
Lollipop Dragon's Valentine Party

Katharine Hepburn's Tales of Wit and Wisdom
(video)

The Emperor's New Clothes
Jack and the Beanstalk
Musicians of Bremen

Merry Mouse School Days

Learning About ABCs
Learning About Counting and Colors

A Merry Mouse Treasury

A Merry Mouse Christmas A-B-C

*Mr. Men and Little Miss Discover Colors,
Shapes and Alphabet*

Alphabet Match Up
Shape Search
Shopping for Colors
The Night Before Christmas

Rudolph the Red-nosed Reindeer Stories

Rudolph the Red-nosed Reindeer

Safety Adventures of the Lollipop Dragon

Remembering and Using Safety Rules
School Bus Safety
St. Patrick's Day

Seasonal Adventures of the Lollipop Dragon

Summer
Winter

Slim Goodbody's Five Senses

Hear Ye
What a Sight

Slim Goodbody's Health Series

A Healthy Day

Slim Goodbody's World of Weather and Climate

Our Friend the Sun
Water Is in the Air
Whirling Winds

When Dinosaurs Lived

Meat-eating Dinosaurs
Plant-eating Dinosaurs

Walt Disney Videos (available in most local video stores)

Dumbo
Too Smart for Strangers
Winnie the Pooh

Weston Woods (Weston, CT 06883)

Beauty and the Beast
The Big Snow
Brother to the Wind
Curious George Rides a Bike
Hot Hippo
Little Toot
Mike Mulligan and His Steam Shovel
Morris' Disappearing Bag
Stone Soup
Tale of Peter Rabbit
Three Billy Goats Gruff
Where the Wild Things Are
Whistle for Willie
Wynken, Blynken and Nod

Additional Materials

If your budget is generous enough to allow film purchases, excellent short films are recommended in *More Films Kids Like*, by Maureen Gaffney (Chicago: American Library Association, 1977). The following commercial materials are excellent supplements to the *Year-Round Calendar* and are recommended when budgets permit.

•*Vocabulary Development Posters*

•*Oral Language Development Posters*

•*Auditory Familiar Sounds Audiocassette*

•*All-Purpose Photo Library, Set 1 and Set 2*

DLM Teaching Resources
One DLM Park
Allen, TX 75002

•*Math Their Way*

Center for Innovation in Education
19225 Vineyard Lane
Saratoga, CA 05070

•*Peabody Language Development Kit, Level P*

American Guidance Service
Publishers' Building
Circle Pines, MN 55014-1796

Sources of Information About Early Childhood Education

Organizations

Association for Childhood Education
International
1141 Georgia Avenue, Suite 200
Wheaton, MD 20902
Publication: *Childhood Education*

Child Care Information Exchange
P.O. Box 2890
Redmond, WA 98073
Publication: *Exchange*

Children's Defense Fund
112 C Street, NW
Washington, DC 20001

Child Welfare League of America
440 First Street, NW, Suite 310
Washington, DC 20001
Publication: *Child Welfare*

Council for Exceptional Children
1920 Association Drive
Reston, VA 22091
Publication: *Exceptional Children*

Educational Resources Information Center on
Elementary and Early Childhood Education
(ERIC/ECE)
805 West Pennsylvania Avenue
Urbana, IL 61801
Publications: *ERIC/ECE Bulletin*, *Early
Childhood Research Quarterly*

National Association for Creative Children
and Adults
8080 Spring Valley Drive
Cincinnati, OH 45236
Publication: *The Creative Child and Adult*

National Association for the Education of
Young Children (NAEYC)
1834 Connecticut Avenue, NW
Washington, DC 20009
Publication: *Young Children*

National Institute of Child Development
North Texas State University
P.O. Box 13857
Denton, TX 76209-3857

Society for Research in Child Development
5720 South Woodlawn
Chicago, IL 60367
Publication: *Child Development*

U.S. Department of Health and Human
Services
Administration for Children, Youth and
Family
Washington, DC 20201
Publication: *Children Today*

World Organization for Preschool Education
P.O. Box 3378
Tel Aviv 61033
Israel

Magazines for Children

Children's Playmate
Saturday Evening Post Company
1100 Waterway Boulevard
P.O. Box 567 B
Indianapolis, IN 46206
(Ages 5–7)

Highlights for Children
2300 West Fifth Avenue
P.O. Box 269
Columbus, OH 43272
(Preschool and elementary)

Humpty Dumpty's Magazine
1100 Waterway Boulevard
P.O. Box 567
Indianapolis, IN 46206
(Ages 4–6)

Let's Find Out
Scholastic Classroom Magazines
2931 E. McCarty Street
P.O. Box 3710
Jefferson City, MO 65102-9957
(Prekindergarten and kindergarten)

My Own Magazine
General Learning Corporation
60 Revere Drive
Northbrook, IL 60062-1563
(Ages 3–6)

Scienceland
501 Fifth Avenue, Suite 2108
New York, NY 10017
(Preschool and elementary)

Sesame Street Magazine
Children's Television Workshop
One Lincoln Plaza
New York, NY 10023
(Ages 2–6)

Turtle Magazine for Preschool Kids
Children's Better Health Institute
1100 Waterway Boulevard
P.O. Box 567
Indianapolis, IN 46206
(Ages 2–5)

Wee Wisdom
Unity School of Christianity
Unity Village, MO 64065
(Preschool through elementary)

Wow
Scholastic Magazines, Inc.
730 Broadway
New York, NY 10003
(Preschool through elementary)

Your Big Backyard
National Wildlife Federation
1412 16th Street, NW
Washington, DC 20036-2266

Magazines for Educators

Beginnings, The Magazine for Teachers of Young Children
P.O. Box 2890
Redmond, WA 98703

Day Care and Early Education
Human Services Press, Inc.
72 Fifth Avenue
New York, NY 10011

Early Childhood Teacher
7500 Old Oak Boulevard
Cleveland, OH 44130

First Teacher
P.O. Box 29
60 Main Street
Bridgeport, CT 06602

Growing Child
Dunn & Hargitt, Inc.
22 North Second Street
Lafayette, IN 47902

International Journal of Early Childhood
28 Stuart Road
Herts, EN4 8X6
United Kingdom

Pre-K Today
Scholastic, Inc.
P.O. Box 7501
2931 East McCarty Street
Jefferson City, MO 65102-9957

Totline
Warren Publishing House, Inc.
P.O. Box 2255
Everett, WA 98203

References and Recommended Readings

Almy, Millie. *The Early Childhood Educator at Work.* New York, NY: McGraw-Hill, 1975.

Anderson, Robert H., and Harold Shane, eds. *As the Twig Is Bent.* Boston: Houghton Mifflin, 1971.

Attermeier, Susan M., Kenneth G. Jens, and Nancy Johnson-Martin. *The California Curriculum for Handicapped Infants and Infants at Risk.* Baltimore: Paul H. Brookes, 1986.

Audin, Neva, et al. *Sliver Budett Music: Early Childhood.* Morristown, NJ: Silver Burdett, 1981.

Bagnato, Stephen J., and John T. Neisworth. *Linking Developmental Assessment and Curricula Prescriptions for Early Intervention.* Rockville, MD: Aspen Systems, 1981.

Bangs, Tina E. *Language and Learning Disorders of the Preacademic Child.* Englewood Cliffs, NJ: Prentice-Hall, 1982.

Bauer, Caroline Feller. *This Way to Books.* Bronx, NY: H.W. Wilson, 1983.

Bayless, Kathleen M., and Marjorie E. Ramsey. *Kindergarten Programs and Practices.* St. Louis, MO: C. V. Mosby, 1980.

Beall, Pamela, and Susan Nipp. *Wee Sing.* Los Angeles: Price/Stern/Sloan, 1985.

——. *Wee Sing and Play.* Los Angeles: Price/Stern/Sloan, 1981.

——. *Wee Sing Around the Campfire.* Los Angeles: Price/Stern/Sloan, 1983.

——. *Wee Sing Children's Songs and Fingerplays.* Los Angeles: Price/Stern/Sloan, 1986.

Bee, Helen. *The Developing Child.* New York, NY: Harper & Row, 1978.

Bell, Sally Claster, and Dolly Langdon. *Romper Room's Miss Sally Presents 200 Fun Things to Do with Little Kids.* Garden City, NY: Doubleday, 1983.

Berg, Richard C. *Music for Young Americans, Kindergarten Edition.* Lancaster, TX: American Book, 1959.

Bergan, John, and Ronald Henderson. *Child Development.* Columbus, OH: Charles Merrill, 1979.

Bertail, Inez, ed. *Complete Nursery Song Book.* New York, NY: Lothrop, Lee and Shepard, 1947.

Blay, Edgar S. *The Best Singing Games for Children of All Ages.* New York, NY: Sterling, 1957.

Bloom, Benjamin S. *Stability and Change in Human Characteristics.* New York, NY: John Wiley, 1964.

Broman, Betty L. *The Early Years in Childhood Education.* Chicago, IL: Rand McNally, 1978.

Brown, Mona. *Projects and Ideas for the Kindergarten Calendar.* Minneapolis, MN: T. S. Denison, 1978.

Buros, Oscar K. *The Eight Mental Measurements Yearbook.* Highland Park, NJ: Gryphon, 1978.

Burton, Leon, and Kathy Kurode. *Arts Play.* Menlo Park, CA: Addison-Wesley, 1981.

Campbell, A. Anne, and Alton D. Quick. *Lesson Plans for Enhancing Preschool Developmental Progress.* Dubuque, IA: Project MEMPHIS, Kendall/Hunt, 1976.

Champlin, John, and Connie Champlin. *Books, Puppets and the Mentally Retarded Student.* Omaha, NE: Special Literature Press, 1981.

Chenfield, Mimi Brodsky. *Creative Activities for Young Children.* New York, NY: Harcourt Brace Jovanovich, 1983.

Cherry, Clare. *Creative Movement for the Developing Child.* Belmont, CA: Fearon/David S. Lake, 1971.

Cherry, Clare, Barbara Harkness, and Kay Kuzma. *Nursery School and Day Care Center Management Guide,* 2d ed. Belmont, CA: Fearon/David S. Lake, 1987.

Cochran, Norman A., et al. *Learning on the Move: An Activity Guide for Preschool Parents and Teachers.* Dubuque, IA: Kendall/Hunt, 1975.

Cohen, Dorothy H., and Marguerita Rudolph. *Kindergarten and Early Schooling.* Englewood Cliffs, NJ: Prentice-Hall, 1977.

Croft, Doreen, and Robert Hess. *An Activity Handbook for Teachers of Young Children,* 3d ed. Cambridge, MA: Houghton Mifflin, 1980.

Croswell, Liz, and Dixie Hibner. *Finger Frolics.* Livonia, MI: Partner Press, 1980.

Dallin, Leon, and Robert W. Winslow. *Music Skills for Classroom Teachers.* Dubuque, IA: William Brown, 1964.

Davidson, Tom. *The Learning Center Book: An Integrated Approach.* Santa Monica, CA: Goodyear, 1976.

References and Recommended Readings

Decker, Celia Anita, and John R. Dicker. *Planning and Administrating Early Childhood Programs.* Columbus, OH: Charles Merrill, 1976.

Delamar, Gloria. *Children's Rhymes and Rhythms: Children's Counting-Out Rhymes, Fingerplays, Jump-Rope and Bounce-Ball Chants and Other Rhythms.* Jefferson, NC: McFarland, 1983.

Division of Special Education (Eugene C. Pratt, director). *Early Childhood Handicapped Resource Guide.* Elkader, IA: Keystone Area Education Agency, 1964.

———. *Preschool Curriculum for Exceptional Children.* Elkader, IA: Keystone Area Education Agency, 1975.

Donoghue, Mildred R. *The Child and the English Language Arts.* Dubuque, IA: William C. Brown, 1979.

Edge, Nellie, and Pierre M. Leitz. *Kids in the Kitchen.* Port Angeles, WA: Peninsula, 1975.

Eliason, Claudia, and Loa Jenkins. *A Practical Guide to Early Childhood Curriculum.* St. Louis, MO: C. V. Mosby, 1977.

Ellis, Mary Jackson. *The Kindergarten Log, Vol. II.* Minneapolis, MN: T. S. Denison, 1960.

Fallen, Nancy, H., and Jill E. McGovern. *Young Children with Special Needs.* Columbus, OH: Charles Merrill, 1978.

Ferguson-Florissant School District. *Holiday Games Developed by Classroom Teachers.* 1005 Waterford Dr., Florissant, MO 63033: Ferguson-Florissant School District, 1985.

Findlay, Jane, et al. *A Planning Guide to the Preschool Curriculum.* Winston-Salem, NC: Kaplan Press, 1976.

Flemming, Bonnie Mack, and Darlene Hamilton. *Resources for Creative Teaching— Early Childhood Education.* New York, NY: Harcourt Brace Jovanovich, 1977.

Forman, George E., and Fleet Hill. *Constructive Play—Applying Piaget in the Preschool.* Menlo Park, CA: Addison-Wesley, 1984.

Frank, Marjorie. *I Can Make a Rainbow.* Nashville, TN: Incentive, 1976.

Glazer, Tom. *Do Your Ears Hang Low?* Garden City, NY: Doubleday, 1980.

———. *Eye Winker, Tom Tinker, Chin Chopper: Fifty Musical Fingerplays.* Garden City, NY: Doubleday, 1973.

———. *Music for Ones and Two.* Garden City, NY: Doubleday, 1983.

Golubchick, Leonard H., and Barry Persky, eds. *Early Childhood Education.* Wayne, NJ: American Federation of Teachers, Avery Publishing Group, 1977.

Good, Linda. *Curriculum from A to Z.* Minneapolis, MN: T. S. Denison, 1984.

Grayson, Marion, and Nancy Weyl. *Let's Do Fingerplays.* Washington, DC: Robert B. Luce, 1962.

Hanna, Rosemarie, et al. *Developmental Communication Curriculum Activity Handbook.* Columbus, OH: Bell and Howell, 1982.

Harrop, Beatrice. *Okki-tokki-unga: Action Songs for Children.* London, England: A & C Black, 1976.

Hart, Jane. *Singing Bee: A Collection of Favorite Children's Songs.* New York, NY: Lothrop, Lee and Shepard, 1982.

Hendrick, Joanne. *Total Learning for the Whole Child.* St. Louis, MO: C. V. Mosby, 1980.

———. *The Whole Child: New Trends in Early Education.* St. Louis, MO: C. V. Mosby, 1975.

High-Scope. *Young Children in Action.* Ypsilanti, MI: High-Scope Press, 1979.

Hoffman, James, and Joan Hoffman. *Prekindergarten Discoveries.* Minneapolis, MN: T. S. Denison, 1986.

Hunt, Tamara, and Nancy Renfro. *Puppetry in Early Childhood Education.* Austin, TX: Nancy Renfro Studios, 1982.

Indenbaum, Valerie, and Marcia Shapiro. *The Everything Book for Teachers of Young Children.* Livonia, MI: Partner Press, 1983.

Jenkins, Ella. *The Ella Jenkins Songbook.* New York, NY: Oak, 1966.

Jenkins, Gladys, and Helen Shacter. *These Are Your Children.* Glenview, IL: Scott Foresman, 1975.

Joliet Public Schools District 86. *Activity Book for Kindergarten Curriculum.* Joliet, IL: Joliet Public Schools District 86, 1970.

Karnes, Merle B., ed. *The Underserved: Our Young Gifted Children.* Reston, VA: ERIC, Council for Exceptional Children, 1983.

Keefe, Betty. *Fingerpuppets, Fingerplays and Holidays.* Omaha, NE: Special Literature Press, 1984.

Keegan, Rosemary. *Readiness Adventures.* Chicago: Follett, 1966.

Kirchners, Audrey Brine. *Basic Beginnings: A Handbook of Learning Games and Activities.* Washington, DC: Acropolis, 1980.

References and Recommended Readings

Kohls, Robert. *Your Art Idea Book.* Dansville, NY: F. A. Owen, 1965.

Labinowicz, Ed. *The Piaget Primer: Thinking Learning Teaching.* Menlo Park, CA: Addison-Wesley, 1980.

Landreth, Catherine. *Preschool Learning and Teaching.* New York, NY: Harper & Row, 1972.

Leighton, Audrey Olson. *Fingerplay Friends: Action Rhymes for Home, Church and School.* Valley Forge, PA: Judson, 1984.

Lewis, Rena B., and James A. McLoughlin. *Assessing Special Students, Strategies and Procedures.* Columbus, OH: Charles Merrill, 1981.

Lillie, David L. *Early Childhood Education: An Individualized Approach to Developmental Instruction.* Chicago: Science Research Associates, 1975.

MacKenzie, Collier Forte. *Kids' Stuff: Kindergarten and Nursery School.* Nashville, TN: Incentive, 1969.

Manburg, Abbey, and Marilyn Segal, eds. *Nova University Curriculum All About Child Care.* Ft. Lauderdale, FL: Nova University Press, 1981.

Marzollo, Jean. *The Big Fearon Early Learning Book.* Belmont, CA: Fearon Teacher Aids/David S. Lake, 1981.

Maxim, George W. *The Very Young: Guiding Children from Infancy Through the Early Years.* Belmont, CA: Wadsworth, 1985.

Mayesky, Mary, et al. *Creative Activities for Young Children.* Albany, NY: Delmar, 1985.

Mitchell, Donald, and Carey Blyton. *Every Child's Book of Nursery Songs.* New York, NY: Bonanza, 1968.

Moore, Vardine. *Preschool Story Hour.* Metuchen, NJ: Scarecrow, 1972.

Mourouzis, Ann, et al. *Body Management Activities.* Cedar Rapids, IA: Missen, 1970.

Myers, Celeste, ed. *Live Oak Curriculum Circle Preschool Project.* Piedmont, CA: Live Oak Preschool Project, 1976.

National Association for the Education of Young Children. "Position Statement on Developmentally Appropriate Practice in Programs for 4- and 5-Year-Olds." *Young Children* (September 1986).

Nelson, Esther. *The Funny Song Book.* New York, NY: Sterling, 1984.

———. *The Silly Song Book.* New York, NY: Sterling, 1982.

———. *Singing and Dancing Games for the Very Young.* New York, NY: Sterling, 1982.

Newmann, Dana. *The Early Childhood Teachers Almanack.* West Nyack, NY: Center for Applied Research in Education, 1984.

Olive, Jane, and Allen Mori. *Handbook of Preschool Special Education.* Rockville, MD: Aspen Systems, 1980.

Olson, Marcia, ed. *Kindergarten . . . A Year of Beginnings.* Des Moines, IA: Department of Public Instruction, 1979.

Oppenheim, Joanne F. *Kids and Play.* New York, NY: Bank Street College of Education/Ballantine, 1984.

Palmer, Hap. *Songs for Learning Through Music and Movement.* Sherman Oaks, CA: Alfred Publishing Company, 1981.

Pillsbury Kitchens' Family Cookbook. Minneapolis, MN: Pillsbury, 1979.

Prelutsky, Jack. *The Random House Book of Poetry for Children.* New York, NY: Random House, 1983.

———. *Read-Aloud Rhymes for the Very Young.* New York, NY: Knopf, 1986.

Purdy, Susan Gold. *Jewish Holiday Cookbook.* New York, NY: Franklin Watts, 1979.

Quackenbush, Robert. *The Holiday Songbook.* New York, NY: Lothrop, Lee and Shepard, 1977.

Raffi. *The Raffi Singable Song Book.* New York. NY: Crown, 1980.

Rather, Louis, and Mildred Swift. *Kindergarten Science.* Minneapolis, MN: T. S. Denison, 1964.

Read, Katherine, and June Patterson. *The Nursery School and Kindergarten: Human Relationships and Learning.* New York, NY: Holt, Rinehart and Winston, 1980.

Robinson, Cordelia, Kathleen B. Davey, and Linda Esterling. *A Review and Catalog of Early Childhood Special Education Resources.* Omaha, NE: Myer Children's Rehabilitation Institute, University of Nebraska Medical Center, 1982.

Rockwell, Robert E., et al. *Hug a Tree.* Mt. Ranier, MD: Gryphon, 1985.

Rogovin, Anne. *Let Me Do It.* Scranton, PA: Harper & Row, 1980.

Sanford, Anne, et al. *A Planning Guide to the Preschool Curriculum,* rev. ed. Winston-Salem, NC: Chapel Hill Training-Outreach Project, 1983.

References and Recommended Readings

Schickedanz, Judith, et al. *Strategies for Teaching Young Children.* Englewood Cliffs, NJ: Prentice-Hall, 1977.

Scott, Louise Binder, and J. J. Thompson. *Rhymes for Fingers and Flannelboards.* Minneapolis, MN: T. S. Denison, 1984.

Shakesby, Paul S. *Child's Work.* Edited by Peter J. Dorman. Philadelphia: Running Press, 1974.

Spizman, Robyn Freedman. *Lollipop Grapes and Clothespin Critters.* Menlo Park, CA: Addison-Wesley, 1985.

Streets, Donald T. *Administering Day Care and Preschool Programs.* Boston: Allyn and Bacon, 1982.

Stuart, Frances. *Classroom Activities.* Washington, DC: American Association for Health, PE, and Recreation, 1966.

Swanson, H. Lee, and Billy L. Watson. *Educational and Psychological Assessment of Exceptional Children: Theories, Strategies and Applications.* St. Louis, MO: C. V. Mosby, 1982.

Toole, Amy, and Ellen Boehm. *Off to a Good Start.* New York, NY: Walker, 1983.

Valett, Robert E. *The Remediation of Learning Disabilities.* Belmont, CA: Fearon Teacher Aids/David S. Lake, 1967.

Voake, Charlotte. *Over the Moon: A Book of Nursery Rhymes.* New York, NY: Clarkson Potter, 1985.

Weiss, Ellen. *Things to Make and Do for Christmas.* New York, NY: Franklin Watts, 1980.

Weiss, Nicki. *If You're Happy and You Know It.* New York, NY: Greenwillow, 1987.

Wilmes, Dick, and Liz Wilmes. *The Circle Time Book for Holidays and Seasons.* Dundee, IL: Building Blocks, 1982.

Winn, Marie, and Alan Miller. *The Fireside Book of Children's Songs.* New York, NY: Simon and Schuster, 1966.

Winslow, Robert W., and Leon Dallin. *Music Skills for Classroom Teachers,* 2d ed. Dubuque, IA: William C. Brown, 1964.

Wolfe, Irving W., et al. *Music Around Us.* Chicago: Follett, 1964.

Index of Skills

The skills are organized by traditional subject areas in order to show how they relate to the skills taught in primary school. The skills highlighted each week are shown at the top of each calendar page under the heading "Skills to Introduce."

Science (S)	Weeks Highlighted
• Name and describe uses of body parts	Sept 2, Sept 3, Sept, 4, Oct 1, Jun, 1
• Distinguish between healthy and junk foods	Nov 3, Feb 3, Mar 3
• Categorize common foods	Nov 3, Nov 4, Mar 3
• Describe weather, using terms such as sunny, rainy, cold	Oct 3, Jan 1, Jan 2, Mar 2, May 4, Aug 4
• Identify seasonal changes	Oct 3, Jan 1, Apr 1, May 4
• Name necessary elements for plant growth	Apr 1, Apr 4, Jul 2
• Identify basic parts of a plant	Oct 3, Apr 1, Apr 4
• Identify and name pets and farm, circus, and zoo animals	Dec 1, Mar 1, Apr 3, May 3, Jul 4
• Discriminate animal sounds	Dec 1, Mar 1, Apr 3, May 3
• Identify methods for measuring time	Dec 3, Jan 3, May 2
• Predict changes from liquid to solid	Jan 1, Mar 2, Mar 4, Jul 2
• Measure amounts of liquids and solids	Nov 4, Dec 4, Mar 3, Aug 3
• Name and explain use of senses	Sept 4, Oct 1, Oct 4, Jul 1, Aug 4
• Demonstrate awareness of reproduction	Apr 2, Apr 3, Jul 4
• Discriminate between objects that sink and ones that float	Apr 4, May 1, Jul 2
• Name some elements that make up our universe	Jan 3, May 2, Jun 1, Jul 2
• Discriminate objects tactilely, such as hard and soft, rough and smooth	Oct 1, Nov 3, Apr 4, Jun 4, Aug 1
• Practice good health habits	Sept 1, Feb 3, Mar 3, Aug 2
• Name ways we can help keep our world pollution-free	Apr 4, May 1, Jul 2, Aug 4
• Discriminate between living and nonliving things	Dec 2, Feb 3, Jul 4

Social Studies (SS)	Weeks Highlighted
• Identify emotions and feelings	Oct 2, Oct 4, Feb 4, Jun 2
• Name members of a family	Nov 1, Feb 2, Jun 3
• Describe role of the family	Nov 1, Apr 2, Jun 3
• Identify different types of homes	Nov 2, May 3, Aug 2
• Name buildings and objects found in the city and in the country	Jan 4, Apr 3, Aug 1
• Match common objects found in the home to appropriate locations	Nov 2, Feb 4, Jun 3
• Match buildings and stores to their functions	Jan 4, Feb 1, Aug 3
• Name jobs and workers in the community	Feb 1, Feb 2, Feb 3, Jun 4, Aug 3
• Give reasons why people work	Feb 1, Feb 4, Aug 3
• Give examples and reasons for school and community rules	Sept 1, Feb 4, May 4
• Name and associate objects of clothing	Jan 2, May 4, Aug 2
• Name common holidays and associated traditions	Oct 4, Nov 4, Dec 3, Dec 4, Mar 4, Jul 1
• Identify means of travel	Sept 1, May 1, May 2, Jul 2
• Name methods of communication	Feb 2, May 2, Jul 3
• Comprehend and follow basic safety rules	Sept 1, Feb 4, May 4, Jun 4, Aug 2
• Care for personal needs, such as dressing, eating, toileting	Sept 2, Feb 3, Apr 2, Aug 2

Language Arts (LA)	Weeks Highlighted
• Say first and last name	Sept 1, Sept 2, Feb 4, Jul 3
• State age and nationality	Sept 2, Jan 4, Jul 1, Aug 4
• Recite address and telephone number	Nov 2, Jan 4, Feb 4, May 4, Jun 3
• State gender: "boy," "girl"	Sept 2, Nov 1, Apr 2, Jun 3
• Identify basic body parts	Sept 3, Jan 2, Feb 3, Jun 1
• Identify and name colors	Oct 3, Oct 4, Mar 1, Mar 2, Jul 1
• Select and name opposites	Dec 1, Jan 1, Mar 1, Jul 4
• Formulate questions	Nov 1, Dec 4, Apr 2, May 3, Jun 3
• Use comparative and superlative adjectives	Oct 1, Nov 1, Nov 3, Mar 3, May 3, Aug 3
• Follow directions	Sept 1, Jan 2, Feb 1, May 4, Jun 2
• Name common objects in environment	Sept 1, Feb 1, Apr 4, Aug 2, Aug 4
• Label actions such as running, eating	Oct 2, Dec 1, Mar 4, Jun 4
• Demonstrate understanding of abstract words	Oct 2, Nov 4, Feb 2, Jun 3
• Tell a simple story	Oct 2, Dec 3, Jan 3, Jun 2, Jul 3
• Recognize absurdities in statements	Sept 4, Nov 1, Jan 2, Apr 3, Aug 1
• Recognize objects as same or different	Sept 2, Sept 4, Oct 3, Dec 3, May 4, Jul 3
• Identify object necessary to complete	Sept 3, Nov 2, May 1, Aug 4
• Identify whole picture when only part is exposed	Feb 1, Apr 1, May 1
• Recall and name objects removed from a set	Sept 1, Nov 3, Dec 2, Apr 3, Aug 2
• Associate objects by given attributes	Oct 1, Nov 3, Apr 1, May 1, Jun 4, Jul 2, Aug 1
• Discriminate and identify common sounds	Sept 4, Nov 2, Jan 4, May 2, Aug 2

Language Arts (LA)

	Weeks Highlighted
• Identify rhyming words	Jan 3, Mar 4, May 3, Jun 2
• Recite simple poems and rhymes	Oct 4, Jan 1, Mar 4, Jun 2
• Recall details from a story	Sept 3, Dec 1, Jun 2, Jul 4
• Sequence events from a story	Nov 2, Jan 3, Feb 4, Jun 1, Jun 2
• Locate hidden pictures	Oct 4, Dec 2, Dec 4, Apr 4
• Manipulate laces, buttons, snaps, and zippers	Sept 2, Jan 2, Apr 2, Jun 3
• Demonstrate left-to-right and top-to-bottom orientation	Nov 4, Feb 1, May 2, Jul 1
• Write first name	Dec 4, Feb 2, Mar 2, Jul 3, Aug 4
• Cut along designated line	Oct 3, Dec 3, Feb 2, Mar 2, Jul 2, Aug 1
• String beads, do puzzles, and use other manipulatives	Nov 1, Dec 2, Dec 4, Mar 2, Aug 1
• Copy and create designs with blocks and various materials	Oct 3, Jan 4, May 2, Aug 1
• Follow maze and connect dot-to-dot patterns	Nov 1, Nov 4, Mar 3, Jun 1, Jul 4

Mathematics (M)

	Weeks Highlighted
• Count by rote: 1, 2, 3, 4, 5, . . .	Sept 2, Sept 4, Oct 4, Nov 4, Jan 3, May 2, Jun 3
• Sort and classify objects into sets	Oct 1, Nov 3, Jan 2, Apr 3, Jun 1, Jul 4, Aug 3
• Identify basic shapes	Oct 4, Feb 2, Mar 2, Jul 1, Jul 2
• Reproduce basic shapes	Nov 2, Mar 2, May 1, May 2, Aug 1
• Identify top, middle, and bottom of objects	Nov 2, Dec 2, Jan 3, May 3, Aug 1
• Demonstrate understanding of spatial relationships	Sept 3, Oct 2, Nov 1, Dec 2, Mar 1, Aug 4
• Reproduce a demonstrated pattern	Oct 4, Nov 1, Dec 3, Jul 1
• Extend a demonstrated pattern	Dec 4, Mar 4, May 2, May 4
• Count up to 10 objects	Sept 4, Oct 1, Dec 3, Jan 3, Jun 3, Aug 2, Aug 3
• Compare size, weight, and volume of objects	Sept 2, Nov 3, Jan 1, Feb 3, Apr 4, Aug 4
• Compare sets to determine if they have more, less, or equal number of members	Nov 4, Dec 4, Mar 3, Apr 3, Jun 2
• Match sets using 1-to-1 correspondence	Oct 3, Jan 1, Feb 1, Apr 2, Jul 3, Aug 3
• Order objects by size, length, and so on	Sept 1, Dec 2, Feb 3, Apr 4, Jun 4
• Recognize numerals: 1, 2, 3, 4, 5, . . .	Nov 4, Dec 1, Jan 4, Mar 4, Apr 1, Jul 4
• Match numeral to the number of a set	Dec 1, Jan 4, May 3, Jun 1
• Identify ordinals: first, second, third, and last	Oct 2, Feb 4, Mar 1, Apr 2, May 1, Jul 1

Music

	Weeks Highlighted
• Sing class songs from memory	Oct 2, Dec 1, Dec 3, Feb 2, Mar 3, Apr 3, Jun 1, Jun 2, Jul 2, Jul 3, Aug 2
• Manipulate hands correctly for action songs and fingerplays	Sept 2, Sept 3, Oct 3, Nov 1, Nov 3, Feb 1, Feb 4, Mar 2, Jun 4
• Listen to music for enjoyment and appreciation	Dec 2, Dec 4, Feb 3, Apr 1, Apr 2, Apr 4, May 2, Aug 4
• Explore and create with rhythm instruments	Nov 4, Dec 2, Jan 3, May 4, Jul 1, Aug 3
• Imitate and create rhythmic movements	Sept 1, Sept 3, Oct 2, Jan 1, Mar 1, Mar 3, Jun 3, Aug 1, Aug 3
• Demonstrate understanding of concepts of near and far, loud and soft, fast and slow, long and short, and high and low	Sept 4, Oct 1, Oct 4, Nov 2, Dec 3, Jan 2, Jan 4, May 1, May 4, Jul 4

Art (A)

	Weeks Highlighted
• Work with classmates on group art projects	Oct 2, Nov 4, Dec 4, Apr 1, Apr 4, Jun 2, Jul 4, Aug 2
• Tear and cut paper into approximate shapes and sizes	Oct 2, Dec 3, Feb 2, Mar 2, Jul 3, Aug 3
• Draw and color with various mediums, including chalk, pencils, crayons	Sept 2, Oct 4, Nov 1, Jan 1, Feb 1, Feb 3, Apr 2, Jun 1, Aug 2
• Create pictures with paints, including tempera, watercolors, fingerpaints	Sept 1, Oct 3, Jan 2, Feb 4, Mar 3, Mar 4, Apr 1, May 4, Jun 3, Jul 2
• Use various mediums to print	Sept 2, Sept 3, Jan 3, Mar 1, Jun 4, Jul 2
• Model clay into desired shapes	Sept 3, Oct 1, Nov 3, Mar 4, Apr 3, May 3, Jul 3, Aug 1
• Create constructions using 3-D materials	Nov 2, Dec 2, Dec 4, Jan 4, Mar 2, May 1, May 2, Jun 4, Jul 1, Aug 4
• Paste paper and other materials to make collages	Sept 4, Nov 3, Dec 1, Jan 2, Mar 3, Jun 1, Jul 3

Physical Education (PE)	Weeks Highlighted
• Roll body in coordinated way	Sept 2, Jan 1, Mar 1, Jun 2, Aug 2
• Creep and crawl in various ways	Nov 4, Dec 1, Apr 1, Apr 2, Aug 3
• Imitate different ways of walking: an elephant, a crab, a duck, and so on	Nov 1, Mar 1, Apr 3, May 2, May 3, Jul 4
• Demonstrate ability in ball-handling skills, such as throwing, catching, kicking	Sept 4, Oct 3, Dec 2, Jan 3, Feb 1, Jun 3, Aug 4
• Participate in rhythmic activities, such as hopping, galloping, swinging	Dec 4, Mar 2, Mar 4, Apr 4, Jun 4
• Demonstrate ability to change directions and go around obstacles while running	Jan 2, Feb 2, May 4, Jun 1
• Perform jumping tasks	Dec 3, Jan 2, May 2, Jul 2
• Demonstrate directional orientation by moving to left, right, forward, and backward	Sept 3, Jan 4, Feb 3, Jul 1
• Perform climbing skills on ladders, ramps, stairs, bars	Sept 1, Oct 1, Nov 2, Mar 3, Jun 1
• Use playground equipment appropriately	Sept 1, Sept 4, Jun 3, Aug 4
• Demonstrate dynamic and static balance	Sept 3, Nov 1, Mar 1, Mar 3, Apr 3, May 3, Jul 3, Aug 3
• Participate successfully in games and organized activities	Oct 2, Oct 4, Nov 3, Feb 2, Feb 4, Apr 1, May 1, Aug 1

Index of Games

Directions for the following games can be found by consulting the week noted in the *Year-Round Calendar*. Additional games are described on p.109.

About the Authors

Faraday Burditt De la Camara is presently directing the early childhood program at The American School of Madrid, Spain. She has previously taught English as a second language, preschool, and learning disabled children at the Rabat American School in Morocco. Ms. Burditt holds a B.A. in modern languages and an M.A. in curriculum and instruction. She is the mother of four trilingual children.

Cynthia Holley has 15 years experience teaching in classrooms for preschool, kindergarten, first grade, and special education students. She holds master's degrees in early childhood education and special education. She has served as a consultant to special education and early childhood education programs in the United States and Europe. Ms. Holley is currently a part-time instructor for Central Piedmont Community College, Charlotte, North Carolina. She often field-tests early childhood activities and strategies with her two preschool sons. She is also the author of *Holiday Stories* and *Bilingual Babies*.

Both authors conduct in-service training for the early childhood education program described in *Every Day in Every Way*, and they welcome inquiries.